Ynes Mexia:
Botanist
and
Adventurer

Ynes Mexia:
Botanist
and
Adventurer

Durlynn Anema

MORGAN
REYNOLDS
PUBLISHING
Greensboro, North Carolina

Ynes Mexia

Women Pirates

Women Aviators

Women
Adventurers

YNES MEXIA: BOTANTIST AND ADVENTURER

Copyright © 2005 by Durlynn Anema

Library of Congress Cataloging-in-Publication Data

Anema, Durlynn.
Ynes Mexia, botanist and adventurer / Durlynn Anema.— 1st ed.
    p. cm.
Includes bibliographical references and index.
 ISBN-13: 978-1-931798-67-9 (library binding)
 ISBN-10: 1-931798-67-2 (library binding)
        1. Mexía, Ynés, 1870-1938—Juvenile literature. 2. Women
botanizers—United States—Biography—Juvenile literature. 3. Botanizers—
United States—Biography—Juvenile literature. I. Title.
 QK31.M438A54 2005
 580'.92—dc22

                             2005010694

Printed in the United States of America
First Edition

*Dedicated to all the students I visit in schools—
may they become even more inquisitive.*

Acknowledgments

What a privilege to write this book about Ynes Mexia. The people I have met who are familiar with her accomplishments are thrilled to have her recognized. Mexia is a woman in a scientific field, a Hispanic, and a person who defied her age, starting her career after the age of fifty, when most people think about retirement. She exemplified the power of exploration and discovery. Thank you, Kate Davis, for giving me this idea.

No book is written in isolation, especially a biography. Research is essential and I am forever in debt to those people who provide the research facilities. A big thank you to Michele Wellck, Academy Archivist, California Academy of Science, San Francisco. She provided so much that afternoon, taking personal charge of my research project—and telling me of her admiration for Mexia.

Thanks to others who helped with my research: Denise J. Price, Save-the-Redwoods League; Caitlin Lewis, Assistant Librarian, William E. Colby Memorial Library, Sierra Club, San Francisco; Lori Hines, Photographic Duplication Coordinator, the Bancroft Library, University of California, Berkeley; William Brown, Assistant Director, the Bancroft Library, University of California, Berkeley; and the personnel of the Bancroft Library, University of California, Berkeley, who were so patient with all my requests. The Bancroft Library is the repository for the vast majority of Mexia's correspondence, which represents most of the documentation of her life.

Contents

ONE

A Lonely Life

It would be hasty to assume every great achiever is driven from youth towards the fields in which he or she will eventually excel. Ynes Mexia never dreamed that one day she would explore North and South America as a botanical collector, obtaining almost 138,000 specimens, more than any other woman collector of the era. Her childhood had few adventures and a loneliness that resonated throughout her adult years. She moved often during her youth and found it difficult to meet other people. Yet these challenges enabled her to adapt to the solitary nature of her work in some of the most remote areas of the American continents.

Born on May 24, 1870, in the Georgetown section of Washington, D.C., Ynes Enriquetta Julietta Mexia and

Opposite: Ynes Mexia. *(Courtesy of the California Academy of Sciences, San Francisco.)*

The Georgetown neighborhood of Washington, D.C., in the late nineteenth century when Ynes lived there as a young girl. *(Library of Congress)*

her family remained in that city only a short time—long enough for her to be baptized as a Catholic. She remained a strong Catholic throughout her life, always trying to attend Mass when a church was available.

Her father, Enrique, was the son of General Jose Antonio Mexia, a Mexican general under President Santa Anna and a leader in Mexico's Federalist Party. He was eventually executed for his part in an uprising against the Mexican government. At the time of her birth, Ynes's father was serving in the American capital as a representative of the Mexican government under President Benito Juarez. Her mother, Sarah R. Wilmer, was related to Samuel Eccleston, the Roman Catholic archbishop of Baltimore, where Wilmer had been raised in pampered luxury. She already had children from a previous marriage that had ended in divorce.

Ynes's father, Enrique Guillermo Antonio Mexia. *(Bancroft Library, Berkeley)*

When Ynes was just a year old, her family moved to Mexia, Texas, a town founded on land that had been given to the state by the Mexia family. Located directly east of Waco and south of what would become Dallas, Mexia is in Limestone County. Its layout is typical of the towns in that part of Texas, with buildings surrounding a town square that features a bandstand, where Ynes enjoyed concerts as a child.

Ynes kept to herself and had few friends. Her father was often away on business, so she hardly knew him. Her mother and her older sister Adele were close and constantly together. They enjoyed social gatherings and entertaining friends. Ynes preferred to read or walk into the fascinating countryside. She watched the birds and small animals, and examined the flowering plants. When she was six years old, she began school, which she liked very much.

In late 1879, Ynes's small world changed. Her parents separated. Her father headed to Mexico City. Ynes, her mother, and her sister went to Philadelphia, Pennsylvania. Her mother enrolled her in a private school, where she felt like an outsider. The girls were more sophisticated, having grown up in the city. She could not understand their ways, nor they hers.

Her schooling continued at boarding schools in Toronto and Emmitsburg, Maryland. Each move deepened her loneliness. Ynes found solace in reading and exploring the outside world. She also wrote copious letters to her father in Mexico. Her letters contained vivid descriptions of her surroundings, showing her close attention to the world around her and her careful eye for detail.

When she finished school in the late 1880s, Ynes's father sent for her to come to Mexico City to live with him. Her role in her new home was to supervise a household of servants, all of whom spoke Spanish. She did not know a word of the language, but her father expected her to succeed, and she did. She managed the house and conducted the ranching business.

Ynes Mexia was a loyal daughter, though she and her father were not close. The only time she saw him was

Ynes Mexia as a young teenager. *(Courtesy of the California Academy of Sciences, San Francisco.)*

across the table at dinner—and even those times were rare. Mexia heartily disapproved of her father's succession of mistresses. She never knew what woman she might see in their home—or how long the woman would stay. She learned she had a half sister, Amanda Gray Mexia (nicknamed Amy), and a half brother, Clarence W. Mexia. While never close to her new brother, she and Amy eventually developed a comfortable relationship.

Slight of stature with luxuriant brunette hair and sparkling brown eyes, Mexia was shy and unacquainted with young men her age. According to the custom of the time, she rarely was alone with any man and thus had little interest in courtship. One young man, Herman Laue, a young German-Spanish merchant, persisted in pursuing her. She accepted his proposal of marriage shortly after her father died. They went to live in Tacubaya, near Mexico City, on a ranch she had inherited.

Laue and Mexia had a quiet marriage. He managed the ranch and tried to take care of her, a new role she found hard to accept. She could not have a close relationship with her husband, an attitude developed during an entire lifetime of being by herself. She was not capable of understanding how to meet another person's intimate needs, because hers had never been met. She did try to make Laue as happy as she could because she wanted the marriage to succeed. He died abruptly in 1904 after seven years of marriage.

Now Mexia was truly alone in the world. Her mother and her sister Adele were in the United States, but she had no contact with them. Her half sister Amy rarely visited. She remained on the ranch, taking over managerial duties and running the business. She became an astute financial entrepreneur, a skill she retained over a lifetime.

In 1908, she met and married Augustin de Reygadas. Mexia tried to make the marriage work but she had retreated too far within herself. Her spiraling unhappiness had severe physical consequences, and she would often stay in her room curled into a fetal position on her bed. Her husband was beside himself, unable to understand her.

In 1909, Mexia suffered a mental and physical breakdown so severe her physician advised her to leave Mexico. Her husband agreed, hoping that a move to the United States might help her. He knew her physical problems were a result of mental ones and was happy for her to seek treatment. Her physician referred her to Philip King Brown, a noted doctor in San Francisco and Berkeley, California.

Mexia and her husband lived briefly in a hotel before finding an apartment in the Bay Area. Dr. Brown proved to be the medicine she so desperately needed. At the same time, however, she was concerned about the ranch. She convinced de Reygadas that he must return to Mexico and the business there. Though reluctant, he agreed.

During the next ten years, the couple's main communication would be through their detailed correspondence. She called him "Petsito" and he called her "Petsita." He often begged to come to the United States. Mexia pointed out that he knew little English and had no skills with which to make a living. He unhappily agreed to stay in Mexico.

The study of psychiatry and psychology was only fifty years old when Mexia arrived in San Francisco. Little was known about using prescription medications to treat mental illnesses. Nor were physicians and psychiatrists clear on how mental conditions could affect a person's physical health. Dr. Brown had studied the effects of stress on mental functions and hoped he could help Mexia return to a full life.

Brown showed an interest in all facets of Mexia's activities, something she had never experienced. As their friendship developed, he became the father figure she never really had. She confided to him that she desperately wanted peace of mind. He assured her that it was possible—and she believed him.

This was the first time Mexia had been to the West Coast. She loved the San Francisco area, with its soaring hills hugging the bay and the churning Pacific Ocean. She gained strength by walking the neighborhoods. The city was slowly recovering from the 1906 earthquake, reestablishing itself as the bustling financial and cultural center of the West.

Using the convenient transportation system of street cars and cable cars over the steep hills, she could easily travel the entire city. One of her favorite places was Golden Gate Park, a truly natural urban park. When the

A panoramic view of the Panama-Pacific International Exposition in San Francisco. *(Library of Congress)*

Panama-Pacific International Exposition opened in 1915, commemorating the completion of the Panama Canal, she roamed the grounds for hours. She was fascinated by the Greek architecture, the streams and fountains, and by what had been accomplished in such a short time after the disastrous earthquake.

When she was not seeing Dr. Brown, they kept up a lively correspondence. He recognized her strength of character and encouraged her to find those depths and not rely on others. While their constant correspondence produced letters of encouragement, Brown did not want her to become totally dependent on him. His letters emphasized she should only see him when she had real needs: "I do not think seeing you as a patient regularly is fair to you or me."

Brown suggested she find outside interests, perhaps taking classes that might interest her. Two classes drew her attention—painting and photography. Her art focused on the beauties of nature. While she enjoyed painting, she was more intrigued by photography. As with every endeavor she undertook, Mexia studied every facet of photography and took her camera everywhere. She also continued to write, experimenting in many different genres, from short stories to plays to nature articles.

In 1917, she joined the Sierra Club, attending meetings and going on outings. The outings took her to Yosemite National Park and other sites throughout the Sierra Nevada. The club's emphasis on nature and the environment attracted Mexia. She wanted to be part of

Mariposa Trail in Yosemite National Park. *(Library of Congress)*

this new movement. Through the club, she also began to make new friends. Slowly, Mexia gained more confidence in herself. She found herself more interested in her surroundings than ever before.

Although Mexia realized all de Reygadas had done for her, she knew she could never return to Mexico and her old life. She was also upset at his lack of financial acumen—he was bankrupting the ranch. Theirs had never been a strong marriage, so with reluctance he

Opposite: Mexia waves from a high ledge during one of her trips in the Sierra Nevada. The challenging terrain presented many dangers for those who sought to explore the area. *(Courtesy of the California Academy of Sciences, San Francisco.)*

THE SIERRA CLUB

Sierra Club founder John Muir stands next to one of California's famous redwoods. *(Library of Congress)*

John Muir founded the Sierra Club on May 28, 1892. Its original intent was to be a California association of men and women devoted to the exploration, enjoyment, and preservation of the Sierra Nevada mountain range. Today, the organization's membership totals 750,000 located throughout the country. Twenty-nine offices govern the business of building an environmental community, litigating when ecological interests are threatened, lobbying state and federal legislators, and educating the public at large. The expanded statement of purpose now reads: "To explore, enjoy and protect the wild places of the earth; to practice and promote the responsible use of the earth's ecosystems and resources; to educate and enlist humanity to protect and restore the quality of the natural and human environment; and to use all lawful means to carry out these objectives."

agreed to a formal separation. They remained separated, but records are not clear as to whether they ever divorced. She sold her ranch and took back her name.

The years had taken their toll on Mexia. It was now 1920. She was almost fifty years old and facing an unknown future. Her only certainty was her need to learn.

TWO

Finding a Niche

The benefits of joining the Sierra Club were numerous. Hiking in the outdoors provided a physical outlet for Mexia to strengthen her body. Association with other hikers also gave her new social outlets. Many of the hikers and club members became lifetime friends. And certainly the outings, whether they were day hikes or camping trips, served to trigger Mexia's interest in nature. Often, prominent professors came along to speak about forestry, bird and animal life, and history.

Mexia especially enjoyed the deep quiet of the redwoods. These amazing, gigantic trees have been on Earth for centuries. In the early 1920s, few people traveled the long distance to the northern California coastal area to view them. She could walk among the giants for hours, speculating on how long they had lived.

Groups such as the Save-the-Redwoods League were instrumental in halting the deforestation of redwood trees in northern California. *(Library of Congress)*

But the magnificent redwoods were being threatened, both by the timber industry and by natural disaster, namely earthquakes. This motivated Mexia to become a member of the Save-the-Redwoods League, paying $2.00 annual dues. In a letter to the organization, she wrote, "I am heartily in sympathy with any effort to save these trees, and wish to inquire whether it is only the trees in Humboldt County which are under consideration (to be saved) or groups throughout the State."

Mexia worked with officials of the league, suggesting fund-raising ideas for preservation and recruiting new members for what she considered a worthy organization. An article in *National Geographic* revealed the grandeur of these redwoods to the American public and helped raise funds for preservation. The objective of the Save-the-Redwoods League was to rescue areas of primeval redwood forests from destruction. They also wanted to cooperate with state and national park services to establish redwood parks. Between 1920 and 1928, the league purchased many redwood groves that formed the core of the California Redwood State Park System and later the Redwood National Park.

In 1921, Mexia enrolled at the University of California, Berkeley as a special student. She was fifty-one years old, an anomaly in those days. Only young people attended colleges and universities. Mexia didn't care. She felt education was a lifetime experience and was thrilled to return to learning. Her first course was natural history.

A university expedition led by Dr. E. L. Furlong,

The University of California at Berkeley was a hotbed of intellectual activity in the early 1920s when Mexia enrolled there as a special student. *(Library of Congress)*

curator of paleontology at the university, introduced Mexia to botanical collecting. This introduction to plant life captured her attention as no other project ever had. Mexia had a focus for the remainder of her life: she wanted to be a botanical collector and explore known and unknown places on Earth in search of plant life.

Mexia wanted to immerse herself in the study of plants so she took more courses in botany. In 1922, she joined a botanical expedition from the university to Mexico and had her first glimpse of botanical collecting in the wild. She made only a few collections but could hardly wait to do more exploring.

If a plant is herbaceous, or containing little or no woody tissue, a botanist will unearth the entire specimen. Woody tissue samples, because of their size and weight, usually require a pruner to clip a piece off. In certain instances, plants must be dissected in order to properly identify them. The plants are then pressed and dried, sometimes in the field and sometimes in a lab (Mexia did most of her pressing and drying in the field). Old newspaper can be used to separate the specimens until they are offered to museums and herbariums, where they will hopefully become part of a permanent collection.

When she went to the California Academy of Sciences in San Francisco for additional study, Mexia met Alice Eastwood, an important American botanist. Eastwood provided critical specimens for professional botanists and also advised travelers on methods of plant collect-

One of Ynes Mexia's mentors in botany, Alice Eastwood.

ing. She first studied plants in Colorado's Rocky Mountains while working as a schoolteacher. These studies led her to the California Academy of Sciences in 1892. Eastwood became curator of the herbarium and founded and ran the California Botanical Club. She was able to save the critical foundation of the academy's collection from the earthquake of 1906, but had to begin building once again. Between 1912 and her retirement in 1949, over 340,000 specimens were added to the herbarium.

Mexia felt it was a great privilege to work with Eastwood. During their acquaintance, she would often accompany Eastwood on field trips to the coastal ranges and to the Sierra Nevada. Whenever Mexia had a botanical question, she knew she could find the answer by asking Eastwood.

In 1924, Mexia, with her marriage over and having sold her business interests, cut her ties with Mexico and reestablished U.S. citizenship, which she had given up after her many years in Mexico and her two marriages to Mexican citizens.

Eager to continue her education, Mexia took a course in flowering plants at the Hopkins Marine Station in Pacific Grove, California, on Monterey Bay. There she met Roxanna Stinchfield Ferris, who was going on a collecting trip to Sinaloa, Mexico. She and her husband would be collecting specimens for the Dudley Herbarium of Stanford University. The year was 1925. Ferris invited Mexia to come along.

Mexia was thrilled. Not only would she be returning to a country she knew well, but she would be given the duties of a true collector. She realized one of the reasons Ferris asked her along was because of her connections in Mexico. She would be able to get assistance and privileges not always available to outsiders.

In preparation, she contacted Eastwood with a proposal. She saw no reason why she couldn't duplicate the collection she made and send it to the academy. She assured Eastwood she already had a "good deal of experience in the collecting and preparing of Herbarium specimens," and would forward the specimens directly to Eastwood from Mexico.

Collecting was expensive. The equipment and materials for pressing and drying had to be bought if Mexia was to collect on her own. She wrote another letter to Eastwood in August asking only for expenses. She assured Eastwood that if this was arranged, the entire collection would be the Academy's. Eastwood agreed to pay on a per-specimen basis when Mexia returned.

The trip proved to be a disappointment. Working with Roxanna Ferris was not productive. Shortly after they arrived in Mazatlan, Mexico, Mexia realized that she wanted to collect in her own way and did not enjoy the company of the Ferrises. She had been independent for so long that it was difficult for her to follow the orders and plans of others. The Ferrises agreed she should leave the expedition.

Mexia planned to continue on by herself. She wrote

The Mexican seaside town of Mazatlan. The foothills of the Sierra Madre, where Mexia would soon venture, can be seen in the distance. *(Bancroft Library, Berkeley)*

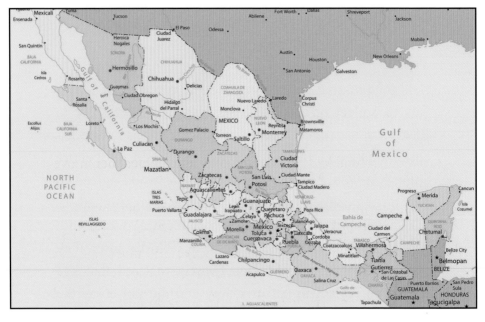

This map of Mexico shows the town of Mazatlan on Mexico's west coast, as well as many of the other nearby areas Mexia would explore throughout her career.

friends in California, asking them to send her equipment. Again, she contacted Eastwood, asking for any help, equipment, or materials the academy could spare. Mexia planned to venture into the hills and mountains above Mazatlan, then down the coast. While the expense of doing this by herself was an obstacle, she was independent enough to realize she no longer could go on expeditions with other people. She felt that going at her own pace into places of her choosing would be more productive.

In the 1920s, women did not venture into unknown regions of the world. A few had explored the wilds of South America—for instance, Harriet Chalmers Adams, Annie Peck, and Mary Blair Niles in the early 1900s. None had spent months in the wild by themselves.

Mexia's wait in Mazatlan for her equipment proved productive. She met a botanist who was happy to advise her about the area around the city. He explained where no collecting had yet been done and helped her move her supplies through customs.

At last, Mexia was ready to explore on her own. She first went along the coast north and south of Mazatlan, collecting coastal forms of every flower and plant she could find. She realized many of these probably had already been discovered but hoped that a few might be new specimens. Then she went into the foothills east of Mazatlan, to an elevation of about eight hundred feet, for more obscure collecting.

Quickly, she realized she had to find a guide. She engaged a native who was familiar with the trails of the Sierra Madre east of Mazatlan. They went on horseback, climbing higher into the mountains. Mexia was fascinated by the starkness of the landscape. She also realized collecting could only be done at certain times of the year—after the rains had come and gone.

Two days later, tragedy struck. Mexia saw a specimen far out on a ledge above a cliff. She was not even aware of her next move; all she cared about was the specimen. She moved ever closer to the ledge. Her determination got the best of her, and over the cliff she went. While the fall wasn't a great distance, it was severe enough that she broke some ribs and injured the hand upon which she landed.

Fortunately, she had her guide. He led her gently to her horse, then helped her into the saddle. In a great deal of pain, she rode back to Mazatlan, where she learned she needed surgery. She had to return to California.

Mexia had obtained nearly five hundred species at the three elevations where she explored, but had hoped for a thousand more. One, the *Mimosa mexiae,* became the first of a number of plant species that were named after her. She had also learned that while she might be fifty-five years old, she had the endurance to survive the collector's rough, lonely, and adventurous life.

Reluctantly, Mexia left the west coast of Mexico and sailed home. As she watched the coastline of Mexico disappear, she vowed that as soon as she was well she would return.

THREE

The First Solo Expedition

A. G. Morton wrote of the study of plants:

> Botany is indeed embedded in human history, from its origins in two of the most ancient sciences of all, magic and medicine, through its long association with pharmacology, agriculture and horticulture, to its part in the exploration of the world, and in ensuring the supply of food and raw materials for the rise and maintenance of modern industrial society.

What began with the earliest human beings as a search for food led to the cultivation of certain plants in the form of crops, then advanced levels of agriculture, and finally the maintenance of livestock. As the use of plants expanded, medicinal benefits of certain species were discovered, largely through trial and error. Plants have since taken on additional significance as beauty and art, as anyone who has seen an orchid or a tiger lily knows.

We enjoy the widespread benefits of botany every day. In 400 B.C., the Greek physician Hippocrates first prescribed for pain relief the bark and leaves of the willow tree, a plant rich in salicin, which ultimately led to the invention of aspirin. Genetic experimentation yielded grass varieties better suited to harsh climates, creating longer feeding cycles for cattle. And we can enjoy an ever-expanding array of breathtaking roses, an assortment that now numbers several hundred.

First-century texts, such as *De Materia Medica* by early pharmacist Dioscorides, account for more than six hundred species used as herbal remedies by the ancient Greeks.

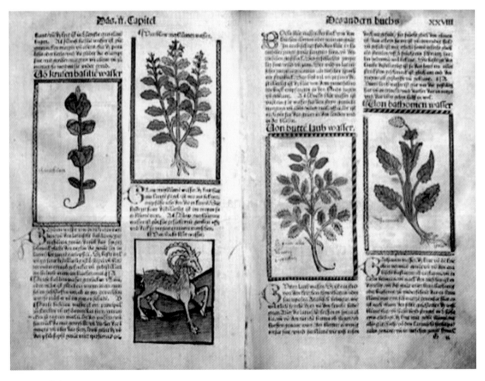

The diversity of plant life is extraordinary. Their shapes, colors, and sizes vary from minute to immense. The scientific division of plants starts at the class level, where those plants with flowers are separated from those without. They can be broken down ten times further according to a variety of botanical characteristics that are used to bring order to the mass of plant life.

Approximately 325,000 kinds of green plants alone have been described. New ones are constantly added to this list. The main reason plants have been classified is to divide those plants that are beneficial to humans from those that are not.

Botanical collectors are a vital part of plant life study. They not only confirm present species and genera (a group of closely related species), but their discoveries might uncover a new plant and/or use for that plant. Serious collection is a rigorous pursuit that takes the practitioner into the wildest of environments.

Horses, dugout canoes, small boats, and foot power were paramount on Mexia's first major collection effort by herself. Although she was collecting under the auspices of the University of California Department of Botany, she needed additional funds. Botany collection is an expensive occupation due to the equipment necessary for pressing and labeling the specimens found. A drier and a plant press must be carried along with materials for pressing the specimens. The prepared collector also brings a compass, pruner, trowel, camera, and any other necessities for survival. All this equip-

Ynes Mexia on horseback, as she often traveled during her expeditions. *(Courtesy of the California Academy of Sciences, San Francisco.)*

ment was a burden. As Mexia wrote after her Mexican expedition, "Transporting of equipment and specimens is a real problem in Mexico, where packing by animals is the only method of getting around, and that often difficult and expensive."

Collecting is also expensive because botanists tend to make several duplicate sets when they collect. They do this so they can distribute their collections to several different institutions and herbariums. While most of the collection goes to institutions in the United States, the collectors also want to include institutions in the country where they are collecting. Duplication also means that collections, which are irreplaceable, are less likely to be completely damaged or destroyed. In addition, duplication ensures that specialists for a particular group of plants will receive and identify their collections, providing a second opinion for identification.

Mexia was able to obtain funds or promises of payment—at twenty cents per specimen—from several herbariums and natural history institutes, ranging from Harvard University to the Royal Botanical Garden. In late August 1926, she left San Francisco on a Pacific Mail steamer. Four days later, the steamer reached the tip of Baja California and sailed east to Mazatlan, the port city of the Mexican state of Sinaloa. From the ship's railing, Mexia could see the fertile inclines of the Sierra Madre.

At the pier, she was met by J. Gonzales Ortega, a civil engineer, amateur botanist, and good friend. She knew "this gentleman knows the west coast of Mexico as few know it, and has been most helpful in advising me as to the best localities for collecting."

Mexia set out by train for Tepic, Nayarit. This quaint old city was in a fertile valley of the Sierra Madre mountains at an altitude of 3,000 feet. This was an advantageous altitude for collecting because it was out of the humid heat of the coast. Despite being on the new Southern Pacific railroad line, Tepic was largely unspoiled by civilization, much to Mexia's satisfaction: "The streets, when not consisting of mudholes, are cobbled and bumpy, with houses and walls of adobe on either side, but the houses are far apart, each set in its garden, or huerta, and the red tiled roofs nestled pictur-

The trip Mexia made by rail from Mazatlan to Tepic covered approximately 173 miles along Mexico's low-lying west coast.

esquely among the tender greenery of the bananas, or the dark glossy green of the omnipresent coffee plants. Even the adobe walls become things of beauty in this ideal climate, for they are covered with a garment of Maiden-hair fern, while above them droop the branches of flowering or fruiting trees."

Ortega had provided Mexia with a letter of introduction to an official in Tepic. With his help, she was able to hire a *mozo* (or guide) named Mauro and two horses. Her fluency in Spanish meant she could communicate with everyone she met. Each morning she and Mauro rode out from the town to explore and collect. She was amazed at the abundance of vegetation, so much "it was hard to know where to begin to collect, and still harder to know when to stop."

Each day, Mexia and Mauro started on a road, then

cut off onto a small trail which led to the higher elevations. Mauro carried the field-press. Mexia got off her
horse to collect and pack away all the plants she could
find within a specified area. Then she mounted her horse
and rode to another location.

Along the way they stopped to eat the wild guavas.
Mexia was amazed at the abundant ferns growing along
the trail and in every ravine: "*Convolvulaceae* of every
size and color were everywhere along the hedgerows
and clambering over shrubbery and small trees, very
ornamental but a terrible pest to agriculturists. . . . The
wild fig-tree, *Ficus mexicana Miq,* here grows to huge
proportions. As the green fruit hung high, Mauro deftly
lassoed some fruiting branches for me."

Usually by three in the afternoon she had collected
all the specimens she could handle. Immediately, she
wanted to get them into the presses to dry them. Mauro
learned how to help her, which she appreciated. Even so,
the task often was not completed until after nine o'clock
at night.

On the trail to the village of Jalcocotan, Mexia en-
thused over specimens that grew wild in Mexico while
gardeners in United States had to nourish them as flowers if they were to thrive. She found cosmos and scarlet
dahlias everywhere. Zinnia, verbesina, and hibiscus
grew wild in the denser wood.

Finding a dense, overgrown trail near Cerro de San Juan,
a spur of the Cordillera, Mexia talked Mauro into taking
it. He informed her it had not been used since the mountain

A sample of Mexia's first new species, the *Deppea macrocarpa*. These shrubs grow in thickets on level ground. *(New York Botanical Garden)*

had been a stronghold for bandits during the revolution. This only made the route more alluring to Mexia.

As they traversed the narrow path, she delighted in the strange and fragrant deciduous trees and the ferns and mosses growing in the dense shade beneath. On their descent the trail was more level and open, leading her to find a new species of shrub (called *pie de pajaro* by Mauro and officially named *Deppea macrocarpa*).

Mexia left Tepic after two weeks of collecting and went southwest by train to Ixtlan del Rio, which was higher into the mountains. She hired a new mozo, Juan, whom she felt was very competent. They rode up the sides of the mountains until they reached the lower fringe of the oak and pine belt. Of the openings of the woods, she wrote, "Many composites were now in flower. On the more sunny slopes we found cacti, among others, a red-fruited *Cereus* [species]. This latter strikingly demonstrates in what manner the slabs lose their spines and shape and become trunk-like as the cactus approaches tree form in age."

Mexia was accustomed to the food of Mexico because of her years of living in that country—she expected to have frijoles and tortillas at every meal. She also appreciated the wild game her mozos often shot and fixed over the open camp fire, but was less enthusiastic about the dried shrimp villagers snacked on like peanuts.

After returning to Mazatlan to deposit her collection, Mexia took a short train trip to Los Labrados and the jungle around Marisma for four days. Returning to Mazatlan, she then went south via train to the village of Ruiz.

The mountains to the north looked inviting. She wished to explore them, but was told to take an *escolta* (guard) if she wanted to go. She didn't like this idea: "I privately think an 'escolta' . . . could be a great nuisance standing around looking at me while I collected and put the plants into my press. I would feel as though I were under guard, but I am terribly intrigued with the idea of the Indians and the mountains. They are not savage Indians like the

Yaquis, just shy and afraid of strangers."

Collecting specimens seemed a limitless task to Mexia. She felt at times neither her materials nor her two hands could "keep up with it. My driers get all filled up and still numberless plants sit and look at me and announce that they are still waiting to be collected. I work to my capacity with what green help I can find in each new locality, and then everyone tells me of all sorts of delightful points to which I have not yet gone, and of all kinds of plants I have not yet come across! It is terribly trying to a greedy collector like myself."

The birds also entranced her. She wished she could have an ornithological companion to identify the multitude of species surrounding her.

A dugout canoe took Mexia down the Rio San Pedro from Ruiz to Tuxpan, still in the state of Nayarit. This river is one of the longest rivers in Mexico, starting in the mountains of Durango and flowing through part of that state into Nayarit before draining into the Pacific Ocean. This river flooded regularly so the surrounding soil was highly fertile alluvial deposits. "Crops (and weeds) grow almost overnight," Mexia later wrote.

From Tuxpan, another dugout canoe took her to Mexcaltitlan. This village of shrimpers sat on an island in the lagoon formed by the delta of the river. Mexia had decided this was a logical place to find new specimens with little difficulty. Dugouts and canoes were the only means of transportation. The river, although broad and swift, was shallow in many places. The canoes were

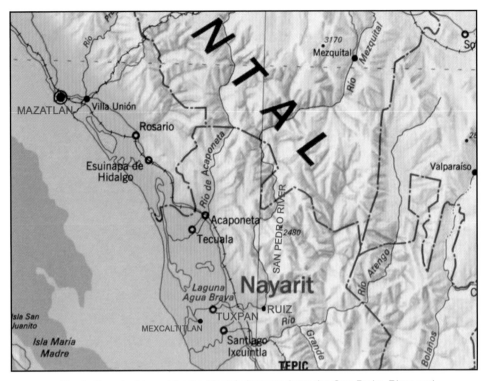

The trail marked in red tracks Mexia's journey down the San Pedro River and through the Sierra Madre to the coastal plains.

hollowed out of a single tree by hand in the mountains, then were brought to the lower lands for sale. In the rainy season, all freight and passengers were carried by these canoes.

Mexia's new mozo, Antonio, piled all her driers and equipment in the middle of the dugout. Then she sat in the prow and he stood astern with a long pole and a broad paddle for the deeper places. Beautiful birds lined the sand banks—black-necked stilts, great blue herons, sandpipers, and even turkey buzzards to clean up the dead animals, birds, and fish. However, she hardly had time to view the birds between collecting specimens and fighting the mosquitos.

As they continued travel, the mosquitos became fierce: "The mosquitos and 'jejenes' (biting gnats) arise from the water in clouds! I suppose they will have an extra good time eating up the poor 'Gringa'. . . . I am instructed to take quinine nightly as a precaution against the deadly mosquito. So far I have had no accidents, illnesses nor anything except bugs and everywhere I have gone, I have been received with courtesy and helpfulness."

Mosquitos were not just an annoyance but also had the potential to transmit disease, especially malaria. This was not the only health risk Mexia took. She had been forewarned of an outbreak of smallpox in Ruiz, so she was inoculated by a doctor in Mazatlan before she left. However, the inoculation did not take. She was not afraid, even though she had never had smallpox—and she never did get it.

As Mexia approached the village, the setting enthralled her. "The village was on a small island in the vast shallow lagoons which stretch along this coast for leagues and leagues. Lovely blue water-lilies . . . grew by the acre and the Corpus Christi . . . lifted its stately white flowers and spread its immense pads in the sunshine. The lagoons, fresh to brackish, were everywhere broken by what looked like wooden islets, which when approached turned out to be association of water-loving trees: Mangrove . . . the Buttonwood . . . *Phyllanthus acidus*, Skeels and others, all growing in the shallow

SMALLPOX

Smallpox is a severe and highly contagious virus-triggered disease that, before its eradication in the 1970s, killed approximately 40 percent of those afflicted. The disease causes extremely high fever and skin outbreaks, incubating for several weeks before making itself known through these symptoms. It dates back several thousand years and routinely caused deadly epidemics until the World Health Organization, with a simple cowpox vaccination and a global plan, eliminated its existence.

Supposedly, only two samples of the disease still exist: one in the United States and the other in Russia, both in laboratories. The samples are maintained in case the disease should reemerge and vaccinations once again need to be produced.

water. In places these trees were so smothered by vines . . . that they lost all tree shape and became but living green mounds."

Her review of the village of Mexcaltitlan was not so glowing: "It was the most miserable little shrimp-fishing village imaginable and I now quite understand why a despicable sort of a person is called a 'shrimp'. You know the type: pigs, children, dogs, mosquitos, etc., all mixed up together and surrounded by an aura of decaying shrimp. My heart sank away down when I surveyed (and sniffed) the village and I began to wonder why I ever wanted to collect in far-away spots anyhow; but there I was and I could only make the best of it. I had a letter to the 'big man' among the village inhabitants and was received with the usual courtesy of the Mexican, be he rich or poor. Their best is always at the disposal of the stranger, yet their best occasionally seems to us . . . pathetically little."

Her accommodation was a back courtyard. She had been offered one side of the room where the family slept, but preferred some privacy. They placed her cot in the yard as far away from a mother pig and ten piglets as possible. However, her cot ended up being beside a hollow where water was thrown out, and each night the pigs grunted and splashed in the water.

A canoe took her out the next morning to collect. Mexia quickly collected all she could from the mangroves, which are water-loving trees. She was fascinated by the landscape: "The lagoons stretch for leagues and leagues and leagues up and down this coast and everywhere the surface of the earth is covered by clear, warm, shallow water. In this area are beautiful, densely wooded islands of dark, glossly-leaved trees, which, when approached are found to be rooted below the lagoon surface, so there is no real land. Narrow, intricate channels wind between these tree clumps and occasionally they fall away on either side forming miniature bays and inlets. . . . the whole is like a beautiful carpet, for the great pads are dull green and carmine, and they form intricate designs over the clear, smooth water, everywhere starred by the blossoms."

Mexia found not only collectible plants but a lustrous

red-bronze bird called a jacana. She was thrilled but noticed her canoeist wasn't impressed. He could only tell her that these birds were very good to eat.

She remained at the village for two days but found little of value. Her return in a canoe was more difficult than the trip down

The distinctive jacana is found in many marshy coastal areas around Mexico and elsewhere.

to the village. It rained steadily and hard. Mexia crawled under the canvas covering her specimens and driers, and endured the snaillike pace.

It became extremely dark, and poling upriver against the current meant progress was by inches. They went aground constantly, at which point the mozo had to get out and shove the dugout into deeper water: "It was eerie enough, the treacherous, unseen river, the heavy, low-hanging clouds, the banks only guessed at by the fireflies' fitful sparks, the occasional glint on the stream of the light from nowhere that but makes the water blacker, the 'plop' of heavy, jumping fish, the long-drawn howling of far-off coyotes, and the unreliable individual with whom I had to deal."

After a weeklong stay in Tuxpan, Mexia was ready to leave the mountains of Mazatlan. Perhaps more valuable than the thousands of specimens she'd already collected was the experience gained surviving in the wild and running her own expedition. Mexia did know one thing: she was ready to explore new areas and discover new specimens.

FOUR

Into the Sierra Madre

The Sierra Madre frame the huge central plateau area of Mexico. Made up of three parts—the Oriental, the Occidental, and the del Sur—the mountains climb from 6,000 to 12,000 feet, set steeply and covered in thick vegetation. Traversing them is no simple matter.

Mexia decided to go to Puerto Vallarta because she heard few collectors had ventured there. Getting to and from Puerto Vallarta was no picnic. The only steamer navigating the route was often overcrowded and didn't make regular stops at this out-of-the-way port. But Mexia was determined.

Dugout canoes greeted the ship upon arrival. Only Mexia disembarked. She took a deep breath as her equipment was unloaded into the canoes, more afraid for it than for herself.

The bay at the beautiful but remote town of Puerto Vallarta where Mexia began her trek into the Sierra Madre. *(Courtesy of Durlynn Anema.)*

She quickly discovered that the rumors about this unsampled terrain were true. The wilderness in this secluded, unspoiled area was immediate, and Mexia only had to go to the end of a small street to collect.

Her collecting habits amused the villagers. They could not understand why this woman, who seemed to have money, climbed the rough mountains. All this, she wrote to friends, was "indubitable evidence [to the villagers] that I must be somewhat touched in the head, but then [they] never know what crazy foreigners will do anyways."

One day Mexia climbed high above the village on a mountain called Cerro de la Cruz, which has a large cross at the top. Her most exciting find was a tree with huge leaves in rosettes called the *hincha huevos* by the natives, who believed an egg coming in contact with any part of the tree would burst.

Among the plants she found was lantana, which was abundant and growing wild. She laughed at this discovery because gardeners in the United States pampered it in their gardens. This was yet another example of how different the environments of the U.S. and Mexico truly were—not only in the horticulture but also in the people and their society.

Climbing around the precipitous hills rising abruptly from the river's edge, she found a small tree later named for her— *Eugenia mexiae Standl*. No matter where she looked, discoveries abounded, until she hardly had enough room to pack all the specimens down the mountains.

When Mexia reached the top of Cerro de la Cruz, she saw the Ameca River

A specimen of *Eugenia mexiae Standl.* *(New York Botantical Garden)*

winding "like a silver ribbon through an alluvial plain forming a short of delta which it had built far out into the bay." She was determined to make a trip to this region. But first she wanted to go even further into the mountains surrounding Puerto Vallarta.

To do this, she hired a man called Pedro, a woodcutter who lived in the hills. When they arrived at Pedro's house, far into the mountains, she was greeted by his wife and nine children. Although they wanted her to stay in their small hut, she insisted she needed to be outdoors. She did this for two reasons: she did not want to impose on their hospitality, and she needed time by herself, something she treasured throughout her life. She camped in a banana grove, which she said was certainly different from the pine trees she was used to in California.

Her location was Cruz de Vallarta, at an altitude of about 2,300 feet. She stayed five days, collecting with the assistance of two of Pedro's boys. The volcanic mountains were a strenuous climb for her. She later wrote that many of them seemed to be "standing on edge."

The boys eagerly climbed trees she felt she could not climb. They picked all the leaves she wanted, although they did not understand why she wanted leaves.

Before leaving Pedro's family, she took photos of them. She realized this seemed to be one of the greatest gifts she could give anyone in this region, because they so seldom saw a camera. Her only regret was that she could not take more photos, but she did not have much film to spare.

Mexia returned to Puerto Vallarta just before Christmas and was thrilled to find a packet of letters from home. It was the nicest present she could receive. She was disappointed to learn that the steamer would not be touching at Puerto Vallarta for some time. She would have to pack out through the mountains. Mexia wanted to collect as high in the Sierra Madre as she could, so she chose San Sebastian as her objective. It was the highest town in the mountains.

San Sebastian was an old silver mining town, nestled in a valley of the same name that rested 7,000 feet above sea level under La Bufa, the highest peak of the region. This valley was just below the frost line, and on the overhanging crests the temperature often dropped below freezing. The mines were no longer profitable to

The eighteenth-century silver-mining town of San Sebastian is nestled high in the Sierra Madre and remains virtually inaccessible by foot to this day.

A dramatic view of the Sierra Madre near La Bufa. *(AP Photo)*

work, so the population had decreased and only a few of the old families remained.

Gazing at the steep, jagged mountains, Mexia knew she would have some rugged hiking ahead of her. Many narrow, deep canyons, made by the streams tumbling down from the crests, cut through the mountains. The canyons were crowded with deciduous trees and shrubs, while the slopes and crests were clothed with pine and oak forests: "The varieties of oak are legion, among them some of the largest and most stately oaks it has been my fortune to see. The pines are also of many species, all that I found but one, being five-needled, and quite different in habit from those of more northern climes. They have not the pyramidal form so marked in our conifers but are quite umbrella-shaped with spreading branches and mostly open foliage, the very slender flexible needles fully fifteen inches long. The tufts of needles ripple in the breeze and catch the glint of the sunshine as our shorter-leaved pines cannot do."

From San Sebastian, Mexia climbed higher to the remains of an ancient mining village, El Real Alto.

"Talk about the primitive!" she wrote from the village. "I am beyond electric lights, beyond kerosene lamps, beyond candles, beyond even dips [sic], and writing by the light of a fat pine torch! And the funny part of it is that it gives a very good light, so our ancestors were not so badly off, after all. Better than that, it gives off appreciable heat also, which as I am on the roof of this part of the world, is . . . very welcome."

El Real Alto was bright and warm in the sunshine during the day. But when the sun dropped into the west, the chill crept in and the nights were bitterly cold. The Indians put out water in little wooden troughs during the day. At night it froze solid, at which point they carried it down the mountainside to San Sebastian to make ice cream.

El Real Alto was built by the Spaniards in the 1500s because of the silver mines in the surrounding countryside. The mines were in continual production until the early 1900s, when the decrease in the price of silver made them unprofitable. The people remaining there hoped the mines once again would open.

The first day there, Mexia and her mozo, Jose, climbed Bufa. The climb was not easy, but she was unafraid, even at "two or three ticklish places." When they reached the peak, her effort was rewarded. The view included the mountains around them, the valley of San Sebastian, and the town below, which looked toy sized. Beyond that was the Pacific Ocean. Following custom, Mexia inscribed her name on the book of ascents, a record of all who had reached the peak. In this case her record was engraved on the broad leaves of a live maguey, or agave plant, which grows in very arid conditions, much like a cactus. The maguey clings to rocks and is used in over one hundred products.

A steep slope towards the south—so steep that no cattle had been there—proved to be thick with interesting vegetation. The oak trees were thickly covered with orchids: "Some very prickly, thistle-like plants filled my fingers with little spines. On the peak, a milkweed grew highest of all the herbs, and a number of the mints were in flower in lilac and blue and scarlet."

Collecting and drying became so fascinating that Mexia and Jose lost track of time. Jose kept saying they never would find their way in the dark because of the faint trail.

Mexia later said, "I did not know I could go down-hill so fast!"

They reached El Real Alto after dark and were greeted by a relieved Guadalupe, Mexia's host in San Sebastian,

Ynes Mexia pressing specimens at her collecting table during one of her expeditions. *(Courtesy of the California Academy of Sciences, San Francisco.)*

who thought they were lost. Guadalupe's concern impressed Mexia. She commented several times during her Mexican travels that everyone she met was so cheerful and hospitable in spite of their stark poverty. Mexia had lived in Mexico for years but had not traveled into the mountains. While she had appropriate clothing and bedding, she noted that the family shivered under a thin cotton tablecloth at night, all huddled together. Many families could not even buy frijoles, except for a treat, and had to eat tortillas for every meal, with no meat at all. She tried to help them as much as she could, amazed at how they wanted to share with her when they had nothing.

After spending five days in El Real Alto, Mexia and

Jose returned to San Sebastian. She sorted and labeled her specimens, and readied them for sending home. However, she missed El Real Alto and decided to return for another collecting round.

On February 27, Mexia and Jose returned to the tiny village. This time it was much colder, and she wished she had brought more warm clothing, especially at night. Each morning, she welcomed the warmth of the first sunlight and readied for a day of collecting: "It is a great wilderness to explore, the tiny trail at our feet the only visible reminder of man, and it is so friendly and inviting, not stark and forbidding and awesome as our more northern mountains often are and I long to wander over it until I am intimate with each deep gashed canyon and each tree-clad upflung peak."

The first few days they stayed close to the village area. The stream beds were rocky and dry. Mexia wished they could find a stream with real water in it, not just rocky outcroppings of former streams. The villagers told her about such a stream, El Jaguey, that was only two to three hours away. They started off early in the morning along the indicated trail to find the stream. This was an area Jose was not familiar with, but he persevered.

By eleven in the morning, Mexia realized they needed water for lunch. They started on a gradual decline that wound around and around as it descended. Twelve o'clock passed. Three more hours of wandering brought them to the brink of a canyon. They looked into a deep gorge in whose bottom they could hear, if not see, running water.

They plunged right down the gorge on a steep zigzag trail. At three-thirty, they reached a cold, clear stream fringed with alders and beautiful willows. Mexia later wrote, "We did not know where we were, but we were definitely somewhere."

Mexia had not been able to completely bathe while in the village, so she took advantage of this opportunity. "It was a 'dip' all right," she later wrote, "for the water was icy and the sun westering, so you can imagine that my scrub, while thorough was hasty to say the least."

After lunch, she began to collect. They had come too far for her to leave without specimens. Mexia found the first alders she had seen in Mexico and some herbaceous plants. She hated to leave when Jose insisted they go. At five o'clock, they started up the slope.

"It grew black night before we were half way home, of course, and many an uphill mile still to go. . . . It was remarkable to me how much better Jose could get along in the dark than I could. I can easily keep up with him in the daytime, but he soon got so far ahead of me that he had to sit down and wait a long time at a herdsman's shack. Then I rather intimated that I preferred he would keep at least within hearing distance."

They couldn't stop in this rocky area. Then Mexia took a tumble in a rocky gully. She hit her shin and tore her ragged clothes even more than they already were. Right after that, Jose fell head first but was unhurt.

Finally, Jose agreed that they must have a light— the night was pitch dark. With his machete, he made two fat pine torches, which made the journey easier. The only problem was that the torches threw out showers of sparks, and in the dry forest that meant they had to keep stopping to put the sparks out, which was time-consuming.

As they saw each familiar landmark they knew they were closer to home. Guadalupe had been close to sending a search party for them when they arrived.

The next day, Jose and Mexia discovered they had taken the wrong trail at the abandoned shack, going five miles out of their way. A few days later, they decided to try again. As usual, the day passed quickly and light became precious as the terrain grew more difficult. At the end of the day, they came to a stream plunging twenty-five feet over a waterfall. Jose decided to work his way up the north wall, clinging to the crevices. Mexia followed him. Then he disappeared.

As she worked her way upwards the walls broke away in rotten rock and loose shale. Every time Mexia found occasional tussocks of coarse grass to cling to, she rejoiced, especially when she heard the loosened rocks crashing into the gorge. Jose kept yelling at her but she never turned around, just kept climbing upwards.

Memories of her previous fall kept her focused on her upward climb. Then she saw a tree jutting out a bit. She pulled herself up on the root and "just hugged the trunk as hard as I could. It was firm and solid, it neither slipped nor gave and never have I embraced a tree trunk with more fervor!"

Mexia scrambled to the next tree and sat down to breathe. She was high up on the slope but on the opposite side of the canyon from Jose. He was hopping up and down and shouting. She could hardly hear him but decided he wanted her to come down the canyon again and up his side. She later wrote, "This I firmly and irrevocably refused to do. I went up that cliff because I got started and could not stop but nothing but the direct necessity would make me go down it."

Jose kept insisting, saying that if she stayed where she was and tried to go on, she would get lost. Mexia agreed with him. Finally, he said he would come to her. She was very appreciative.

Mexia anticipated him picking out an easier route than she had taken. With that in mind, she sat down to wait for him (one arm still around a pine tree). However, when he finally arrived, blowing and puffing, he said he had followed in her tracks. Then he said, "I do not see how the Señora made it." He had slipped twice and thought he was gone (he also was carrying the heavy plant press). He dug toe and finger holds with the botanical pick he was carrying and continued to climb until he made the grade.

It was pitch dark but that did not inhibit Jose's sense of direction. Finally, he found a cattle path and they walked the three miles back to El Real Alto.

Jose was pleased when Mexia said they would return to San Sebastian. He also told her how impressed he was at her walking ability. Members of the upper classes did not walk in Mexico, only the poor. While she wasn't a fast walker, she had a great deal of endurance. He went around boasting of her prowess: "Another like the Señora I have never seen," he said.

With regret, Mexia realized she had to leave San Sebastian with her 33,000 specimens and head for San Francisco. She had grown very fond of the town and its quaintness—but knew she had to take her specimens home for distribution. She was, as always, determined to finish what she had set out to do.

FIVE

The Last American Frontier

Mexia returned from Mexico with nearly 6,600 different plants—lichens, mosses, ferns, grasses, herbs, shrubs, and trees. Included in these was one new genus and about fifty new species, ten of which were determined by the Field Museum of Natural History and six by the Harvard University Botanical Museum. Her reputation as a collector was growing.

On her return from Mexico, she was paid the standard rate of twenty cents per specimen for what she'd brought back, plus additional funds for photographs. Her quality work prompted the British Museum of Natural History to fund a trip to Alaska. Dr. Francis W. Pennell from the Academy of Natural Sciences in Philadelphia promised that, based on the Mexico collection, the academy too would be interested in her yield from Alaska. With these assurances, she was ready to head north.

Accompanying Mexia was Frances Payne, a young botanist paying her own way. She thought it would be exciting to collect with an experienced scientist and learn new techniques. Mexia was honored to be considered so important and proud to become a mentor to the young woman, much the way Alice Eastwood had mentored her.

The women left San Francisco on June 9. They landed in Anchorage, then continued overland to Mt. McKinley Park. This park, now known as the Denali National Park and Preserve, had been established in 1917. Mexia knew no botanist had fully explored the park, giving her an advantage. The summer season is short in this area, making it critical for Mexia to move quickly. She would have only until mid-September before the weather turned.

The 20,320-foot Mt. McKinley, the highest peak in North America, is the primary feature of the park. However, there are over six million acres of additional wildlife to explore. Grizzly bears, wolves, Dall sheep, and moose make their home in this terrain. In 1976, the park would be designated an international biosphere—a laboratory for natural science research. Even before trekking into the wilderness, Mexia was certain she had made the right choice for collecting.

Opposite: This photograph of the intimidating face of Mt. McKinley was taken in the late 1920s. Snow beds cover more than half of the mountain year-round, feeding the region's many glaciers. Mt. McKinley was scaled successfully for the first time in 1913. *(Library of Congress)*

Frances Payne, on the other hand, underestimated Mexia's adventurous spirit. She was not prepared for the rugged terrain and her mentor's willingness to tramp through it in search of the unfound. She quickly decided to stay closer to comfort, near park headquarters. Mexia, no longer so interested in mentoring, quickly agreed to journey on by herself.

The park superintendent told her no person had ever made a botanical collection where she wanted to venture, and added he was "most anxious to have it done." Mexia knew this was an area of nearly 3,000 square miles and couldn't believe she was first.

Transportation became her greatest problem. The railroad stopped at the park, so it was up to Mexia to find a way into the wilderness. Part of the time she hiked, using a few pack dogs to carry her equipment. Other times she carried or hauled the equipment by herself.

Nothing deterred her. The park rangers assured her they would come to her campsites occasionally, but never showed up. She did have some visits from hunters, and even a group of backpacking tourists. But most of the time she was by herself with only her dogs for company.

She faced difficult collecting and hiking conditions daily: "I could only scratch the surface of that vast Park area, but I chose my stations as far as possible from each other and at different altitudes."

Her collection route spanned almost one hundred

miles, beginning at the Savage River, moving to Copper Mountain (as close as she could get to Mt. McKinley), and on to Wonder Lake, a lower elevation that helped her avoid the early onset of snow.

Savage River, at the upper edge of timber line, twelve miles from the railroad and the entrance to the park, was her first collection area. Mexia easily hiked this distance in a day, carrying her equipment so she could remain for several days. Her pack dogs, "a novel method of transportation," worked tirelessly hauling her driers and other equipment.

Collecting specimens proved far more difficult than

Fresh snow dots the tundra along the Savage River in Denali National Park and Preserve (formerly Mt. McKinley Park). The mountain is visible on the horizon. *(National Park Service Photo)*

she anticipated. The roots of the more fragile plants broke off when she tried to dig them out. They were embedded in lichens and mosses. Below the lichens and mosses was an intricate combination of fine woody roots and the underground pliable stems of willow trees.

Mexia tried using a botanical pick. But the pick, she later wrote, "made no impression on this elastic 'wire mattress' sort of growth, for one never seemed to reach real earth, and each plant had to be dug out with a knife, cutting away these roots, and generally getting broken in the process of extraction. I am hardly likely to be up against just that condition again, and so hope for better roots."

The weather presented quite a problem throughout the expedition. Cold rain and wind often prevented her from collecting. Further hindered by the rough terrain, Mexia was concerned that she "only was able to get in the neighborhood of four hundred numbers, possibly not that many."

She wanted to stay longer. However, when it began to snow heavily, she knew she had to leave. Yet, confused by the deep snow, she did not know which way to go. Finally, on September 12, 1928, she and her dogs were rescued from her campsite by an Alaskan on a dogsled.

While Mexia spent the next months working on her collections, she was still anxious to return to the field. She took a minor trip to Mexico in 1929 for three months, visiting the states of Chihuahua, Mexico,

Puebla, and Hidalgo, and collecting over 5,000 specimens. The trip also allowed her to settle some final business issues related to the ranch she had once owned. Her life had changed greatly over twenty years. She'd gone from being a wife situated in one location, essentially running a business, to a globe-trotter who rarely slept in the same place for more than a short period of time.

In 1927, Mexia had met Nina Floy "Bracie" Bracelin when they were both enrolled in a University of California extension course. They became good friends because of their mutual interest in botany. The younger woman looked up to Mexia and her expertise in collecting. However, she was more interested in assisting with the collections than making them. This proved to be a valuable relationship.

There is some speculation about the relationship between Mexia and Bracelin. Both of Mexia's marriages failed, and she never showed an inclination towards romance with another man. Bracelin remained one of Mexia's closest companions until her death, despite their twenty-year age difference. Whatever the nature of their relationship, it was positive for both of them. Mexia was free to devote more time to the field, and Bracelin received a steady stream of specimens to sort and process.

Bracelin had the specimens identified, mainly by the Gray Herbarium at Harvard University. She sorted them into sets and sent them to the various subscribing institutions. She dealt with paperwork, raising funds, and correspondence. Bracelin also transcribed many of Mexia's letters, recognizing the importance they would have in the future.

This left Mexia time to plan her itinerary. After Mexico, she set her sights on the far reaches of Brazil.

SIX

Adventure in Brazil

With each new adventure, Mexia set the bar a little higher. The challenge of an unfamiliar continent could be intimidating to even the most experienced traveler. For the solitude-loving Mexia, it was exactly what she wanted.

Mexia planned to leave for Brazil in mid-October and join Agnes Chase, an associate agrostologist (one who studies grasses) from the Smithsonian Institution, on an expedition west of Rio de Janeiro. But visa problems threatened to ground Mexia indefinitely.

Mexia sent a frantic letter to Chase telling about her visa problems and pleading for help. She realized officials in Washington, D.C., might expedite the process and asked to be appointed as an official assistant to the expedition, which would give her more authority in dealing with the government. Mexia promised in return to collect double specimens, sending one set to Chase in return for this favor.

Mexia's pleas were answered in time. On October 15, 1929, she left San Francisco on a Norwegian freighter bound for Rio de Janeiro. She had letters of introduction to officials throughout Brazil, including the Amazon region. Aware that the populace of Brazil spoke Portuguese and not Spanish like the rest of Latin and South America, she hoped her Spanish would help her translate. This was her first trip among a people in whose language she wasn't fluent. She saw it as an opportunity to learn some Portuguese.

Her departure date was fortunate. Several days later, the stock market crashed, sending the country into the Great Depression, one of the most significant events in this country's economic history. Any later and her trip might have been called off.

As the freighter journeyed south, Mexia relaxed and enjoyed the bracing ocean air. She later wrote, "The trip down to the Canal is a pleasant one; some light rains and all the way down a blessed breeze that keeps us from becoming uncomfortably hot. The sea gets bluer and bluer and the whale is spied in the distance. Land birds are with us, a small owl that looks much like a burrowing owl, a meadow lark and some small sparrow-like birds come to us from the just visible shore of Lower California."

They reached the Panama Canal on October 29. Once

out of the canal, the freighter sped toward the eastern coast of South America, crossing the equator. Mexia thoroughly enjoyed the traditional ceremony for passengers and crew who had never crossed the equator. It took place at the ship's small swimming pool made of canvas and wood, where she swam at least two times a day. People were lathered with paint and soapsuds, then thrown into the pool.

Mexia decided to have a little fun with the ritual: "An imp of perversity prompted me and I thought I would give them a run for their money." She went limp as she was thrown into the water and let herself sink to the bottom. When the scared guards pulled her out and propped her against the side of the pool, she slipped away again. As she pretended to drown, her head went under "as any properly drowned person does." The guards were afraid to grab her, yet more afraid not to rescue her limp body. After they pulled her out, they hesitated again, looking for help. But the rest of the crew was equally scared.

Mexia commented later, "I wanted to suggest artificial respiration but it did not seem to come properly from the 'body' and all the rest were too frightened to think of anything, so after a while I had to come to all by myself without any artificial anything at all, but the joke was not on me this time as it had been with the others."

Mexia enjoyed the trip, especially walking the available deck space and talking with her fellow passengers. The shy little girl she had once been was gone. She could

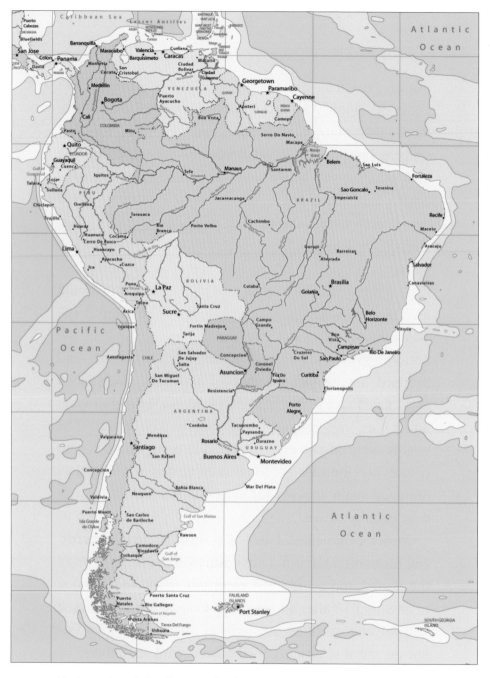

Mexia spent most of her first trip to South America in the north, but she would travel as far as the southernmost tip of the continent before she died.

This bird's-eye-view photograph of Rio de Janeiro was made several years before Mexia's 1929 visit. *(Library of Congress)*

talk with everyone, and felt much more comfortable around people. The monthlong trip was restful, giving her a chance to catch her breath before tackling South America and the adventures ahead.

She met Chase and the rest of the scientific team in Rio de Janeiro. Their ultimate destination was Espiritu Santo, where they would travel into the foothills of Pico de Caparao, the highest peak of the range. This site was chosen because, to their knowledge, no botanizing had been done on the southeastern side.

RAIN FOREST

Tropical Rainforest

Temperate Rainforest

More than half of all species of animals and plants—more than one million—call the rain forests home, despite the fact that rain forests cover only 8 percent of the earth—and this figure is shrinking. The life in these regions provides vast amounts of the world's food, medicine, and fuel. Rain forest plants, through the process of photosynthesis, release over 40 percent of the world's oxygen.

New species are discovered in the rain forests each year. Rain forests exist in consistently warm temperatures, usually close to the equator. Rain falls steadily throughout the year, with cumulative annual totals of more than eighty inches. While they are found in eighty-five countries around the world, 90 percent of the forests are found in just fifteen nations.

They traveled by train to Alegre, then transferred all the baggage and equipment into a truck. The road was muddy, rough, and winding. As they climbed, wonderful mountain views appeared as well as unknown vegetation. The steep slopes were cultivated with coffee bushes, corn, and beans. Growing naturally among this agriculture were cecropia trees, "perhaps the most conspicuous, for they have tall slender trunks with a great crown of huge palmately incised leaves that stand out in a perfect crown showing silvery white on their glistening surface."

The trip proved to be the roughest Mexia had ever taken. Mexia claimed she was unprepared because she "had no idea what it was going to be." She found that Chase, being a "pure and simple" scientist, was "unpractical as all scientists are." Chase even protested when Mexia insisted on taking food for a journey into the wilderness.

On their first day, the group climbed through the rain forest to Pico de Caparao's 9,000 foot peak. There was little available in the way of beaten trails. The constant mist and rain meant all the foliage dripped. They were drenched and had given up any hope of trying to stay dry.

On the first night, their guide wanted to stay under some overhanging rocks. Mexia found the dry earth alive with fleas. She was able to convince the guide and porters to level some ground beyond this place and set up a rough tent. At that point, she discovered Chase had not even brought a change of clothing or warm outer coat, and only a thin blanket. Mexia shared her clothes while growing frustrated at the woman's lack of common sense.

The next day, they continued to struggle upward through the "green gloom" of the forest. They were not thinking of collecting, simply moving forward. Chase's knees became wobbly and Mexia was short of breath. Stops became more frequent. Their guide said it wasn't much farther to the timberline. They finally moved out of the taller fronds into a bamboo thicket and fought their way through the bamboo tangles until they cut through the "green earth drapery" and were above the timberline.

Chase and Mexia were relieved but very tired. Before long, a cold wind sped down from the mountain peaks. Chase's teeth chattered and Mexia, to her shame, became nauseated. They sat at 8,000 feet on the tallest mountain in Brazil. They wondered how it could be so cold when they were so close to the equator. The guide and porters wanted to go to a hut five miles further on, but the women were too exhausted to continue.

They insisted on stopping and talked the men into erecting a type of tent from a waterproof alligator skin and the ponchos Mexia had brought. The men built a fire, then went on to the hut. Mexia and Chase sat inside their makeshift enclosure and ate bread, cheese, and part of a chicken before laying down for the night, listening to the steady rain and howling wind.

When they awoke, it was still raining. They decided they were so wet already that going out to collect would not make any difference. They found so many specimens that they became too involved to notice the time. In the early afternoon, two of the men came down from the hut to try to convince Mexia and Chase to press on. The women declined. They had collected so much that they wanted to put the plants into the press, making them easier to carry.

The men returned at noon the next day. By this time, everyone in the entourage was ready to go to the other side of the range—perhaps to find sun. On the other side, they found a Brazilian family who ran cattle in the hills. The family took the sopping wet group in, gave them hot water, a hot supper, and put them up for the night. The next morning the sun was out, bright and clear.

The group left early the next day for the village of Santa Barbara de Caparao. Unfortunately, the cold, wet weather took its toll on Chase, and she was very sick upon arrival. She decided to rest up in the village for a few days before heading back to Rio. Once again, Mexia was alone, her preferred mode of exploring.

After doing some collecting, Mexia returned to Rio for a few days before her next adventure, traveling to Minas Geraes. She went to the town of Vicosa and visited the state school of agriculture. She found the school a perfect location for collecting. She was impressed to find such a modern institution so far from what she considered civilization: "Out of the, luckily fertile, red clay soil here they have evolved a truly modern institution, with buildings, outbuildings and planting that would do credit to any country in any locality."

The school had been founded twelve years before. There were over one hundred students, all male and all native Brazilians. They learned about agriculture and got hands-on experience with cattle breeding, feeding experiments, and crop improvement. The cattle were large, colored cream to pale gray, with wide-spreading

The campus of the Agricultural College in Vicosa, Brazil, and the surrounding fields where students and researchers worked and studied. *(Courtesy of the California Academy of Sciences, San Francisco.)*

horns and the characteristic hump and pendant dewlap of the zebu. This type of cattle is raised in Brazil because they are useful in both pulling carts and plowing. These cattle can live on dry grass in the dry season and withstand Brazil's very hot weather.

Minas Geraes became Mexia's home for the next year. She divided her time between Vicosa, a *fazenda* (cattle ranch) in the Sierra da Gramma, and another fazenda north and west of Vicosa. These collection localities were in the highlands of mid-Brazil at an elevation of 2,000 feet. This was Mexia's longest journey away from the United States, and she had no intention of returning any time soon.

Mexia benefited greatly from having a local student assistant, Joaquin Braga, who was as interested in botany as she was. Her expedition's caravan consisted of three pack mules, each with two large fiber cases of driers and other collecting apparatus. Three other saddle mules carried Mexia, Braga, and the packer.

Mexia was approaching sixty years of age, but she rarely slowed down. She was amused by the reaction of villagers when they saw her ride onto a main street: "The village was treated to the sensation of all time to see a woman astride. I feared knickers would be too much for the Brazilians, but even a divided skirt was beyond their wildest imagining, and every door and window was filled with, I suppose, shocked spectators."

She still preferred to sleep outdoors to avoid the fleas that seemed to inhabit every house. Her hosts were often shocked by her choice, fearful she'd be attacked by a ferocious beast. Mexia found it delightful.

"To be in a rainforest in Brazil was thrill sufficient," she wrote to friends. "It being high rainforest, one thousand to one thousand three hundred meters, it is not so dense that one cannot see into it, and the great trees, many with lianas equaling their girth, stood above everything. Then the tree ferns are really the most beautiful and graceful things ever created; the stems are slender, showing their leaf scars, and then from the top the great

A Brazilian tree fern.

fronds arch out in most exquisite curves and each is lacy perfect. One thing I was surprised to find . . . ferns are always so smooth and unharming, and the great petioles of these ferns as thick nearly as my wrist, had very decided prickles in the form of recurved hooks not to be trifled with. Why should a fern have prickles?"

Part of the importance of botanical collecting is the insight it can give into how living things exist in the wild and adapt to their conditions. Just as polar bears are white to match their snowy environment, or fish come to resemble the river bottoms they inhabit for protection, so too do plants adjust to ensure their survival.

Mexia's year in Minas Geraes ended with a bang. One night, as she, Braga, and the rest of the porters slept under the stars, a monstrous thunder and lightning storm set upon them. Her team was shaken with the experience.

The next morning, Mexia suggested building a shelter for the men, but they only wanted her to finish collecting so they could return to the fazenda. Braga also had been scared and suggested they collect quickly and then start home that afternoon. Mexia sent the two porters and the assistant to collect a special plant while Braga packed. Although it was not raining, it was cold, windy, and cloudy. Mexia didn't get all the varieties she wanted but did have the press full by eleven o'clock. They were ready to leave by noon.

The group started down the mountain—straight down. Mexia couldn't decide whether this was by chance or by design. They were descending over steep, rocky, waterworn granite. They had to creep along the edges or take advantage of cracks when they appeared.

Mexia later discovered the porters had been so scared by the storm they wanted to get home as quickly as possible. Thus, they took the steep, hard trail rather than the easier one by which they had ascended. Mexia was disappointed, not because of the difficulty of the descent but because she could have collected more plants on the first trail.

After five hours, they reached the level part of the trail and had a smooth hike the rest of the way to the fazenda. While she wished she could have collected more, Mexia realized that aside from the grasses collected by Chase, no collecting had been done in this area. She hoped her collections would encourage more exploring.

A truck took Mexia and her equipment and baggage to the second fazenda. Braga returned to the Agricultural College. Mexia stayed in a large *hacienda* (ranch house) where a housekeeper/cook took care of her every need. The fazenda raised enough coffee, rice, beans, sugar cane, and pork to be self-sufficient. She was appalled that vegetables were never eaten, and fruit only when it could be found. Fifty cows provided milk both for the fazenda and for a commercial creamery. Ten thousand head of cattle ran the thousands of acres, with special pastures for calving cows, yearlings, heifers, and steers.

Mexia was particularly interested in the *vaqueros* (cowboys). Not only did they ride superbly but also

Brazilian cattle similar to those at the hacienda where Mexia stayed while she studied at the Agricultural College. *(Courtesy of Durlynn Anema.)*

handled the cattle expertly. They did not carry lassos but rather long goads or rods topped by a sharp iron spike. These were used to drive or herd the cattle. Mexia spent many hours watching their expertise.

Mexia was excited to find rheas out on the open but mistakenly called them "emus" (both are relatives of the ostrich): "One day I actually had the thrill of seeing three of the great birds at a distance. They were running having probably sighted us first, but even far away they looked huge, and were a sight not to be forgotten."

While she could have stayed indefinitely in the highlands, Mexia felt the need to follow her original dream— to travel the breadth of South America along the Amazon. So she said good-bye to new friends and the beauty of the area and went to Rio to catch a boat to the Brazilian state of Para and the beginning of another adventure.

SEVEN

Up the Amazon

The botanical treasures of the Amazon River, especially at its origin and tributaries, drew Mexia like a magnet. She had dreamed of visiting this area for years: "Most of us, I think, have felt the fascination of the Amazon region. So much have we heard of its rivers, its tropical beauty, its luxuriant forest, the wild life and wilder Indians that lurk in its depths, that the pictures drawn by our imagination are vivid and unique. This vision of the unspoiled wilderness drew me irresistibly."

Mexia spent almost twenty-two months in Brazil before she was able to accomplish her dream. Normally, the Amazon and its tributaries were reached from the west. However, because she was on the east side of the Andes Mountains, Mexia decided to reach the Amazon and its tributaries from that direction. She inquired about the

The Amazon River Basin is comprised of a network of rivers that span the northern portion of South America.

best way to approach these rivers, but because no one had heard of this being done, she obtained no answers.

A lack of information did not stop her. After a few months of side excursions around the north coast of Rio, Mexia booked passage on a comfortable motor ship and traveled directly to Belem, sitting slightly inland from the Atlantic Ocean and near the Amazon's mouth in Brazil. She obtained visas for Columbia, Ecuador, Peru, and Bolivia, because she wasn't sure exactly where she was going. On August 28, 1931, she boarded the steamer *Victoria* for the trip upriver. She was loaded down with equipment in preparation for a long stay in the region.

The steamer was an upgrade in living conditions. Mexia enjoyed air cooled by electric fans and ate fresh meat—"off the hoof"—on this leg of her Amazonian adventure.

As she sat on the deck she absorbed the beauty of the river and its islands. These memories later became part of several articles she wrote: "The river itself is a tawny flood, looking more like an inland sea, 'El Rio Mar de las Amazonas,' than a river. Everywhere it is island-sown, and these islands divide it into *parana* (channels) each of which may be several miles wide. Vessels ascending the river follow these side channels, often bringing the boat sufficiently close to island-shore or mainland to enable one to see many interesting features. Every foot of terra firma is heavily wooded, and these forests of the Lower Amazon are truly magnificent."

The steamer was a wood-burner. Each day the boat tied up at some spot on the shore to obtain fuel to continue the journey. This gave Mexia a chance to go ashore. She was fascinated by the way the forest crowded the settlements of thatched houses, almost hemming them in, with little land left to cultivate. This was not the uninhabited wilderness she had imagined, because the steamer was rarely out of sight of a little settlement.

The *Victoria* reached Santarem, a good-sized town on the mouth of the Tapajoz River, on the fifth day. The huge rubber plantations of Henry Ford were several miles

Opposite: A late nineteenth-century engraving of an Amazon tributary in Brazil. *(Courtesy of the Granger Collection.)*

inland. This area had been visited for years by naturalist explorers, so she was already well acquainted with the vicinity. Most intriguing to her were the open-front stores hung with the skins of huge boas, lizards, caimans, and furs of monkey, ocelot, and many strange beasts.

On the trip's sixth day they came to a town called Obydos. This was the first time she could see both banks of the Amazon. Up to this point islands had blocked the view. When they left the town, she began to see more wildlife—huge *jacares* (caimans), white aigrette herons, and chattering green and silver parakeets.

Mexia enjoyed watching dugout canoes as their single paddler took produce or passengers up and down the river. Whenever the steamer passed a clearing with huts scattered about, all the inhabitants rushed to the shore and waved. The steamer's passengers always cheerfully waved back. Mexia marveled at the houses perched on stilts as a precaution against floods.

On September 2, 1931, the steamer entered the Brazilian state of Amazonas. It soon came to the mouth of the Rio Negro, where the boat turned north into the swift black waters. They arrived in Manaos two days later. This city had wide, tree-shaded streets, electric trams, a hospital, and other modern conveniences. It was renowned for its splendid public buildings and the beautiful opera house of Italian marble topped with a gold-tiled dome. This city in the middle of the jungle had developed because of the productive rubber industry.

An Amazon River rubber boat in the 1920s. *(Library of Congress)*

Worldwide demand for rubber—used in insulation and to make tires for the increasingly popular automobile—was high. Before synthetic rubber was invented in 1930, rubber could be made only from the secretion of latex from rubber trees, found in high concentration in the Amazon basin. In 1876, the British smuggled rubber-tree seeds out of Brazil, establishing plants in their colonies in Sri Lanka and other tropical regions, but the Amazon basin continued to be an important source of this valuable material.

When the steamer continued its journey, it carried a new group of passengers. Mexia was the only continuing passenger. The riverbanks changed, showing sand-spits and newly formed islands. Near the water's edge was tall, coarse grass. Behind were imbaubas, fast-

THE AMAZON

The Amazon River is the world's second-longest river (behind the Nile River in Egypt), running approximately 3,900 miles, or nine hundred miles longer than the width of the continental United States. It carries more water than any river, with an average depth of 150 feet. The Amazon flows through Peru, Bolivia, Venezuela, Colombia, Ecuador, and Brazil before emptying into the Atlantic Ocean.

Until 1637, when the Portuguese explorer Pedro Teixeira led an expedition, the river hadn't been explored in its entirety by nonnatives. The river proved to be important to many scientists and naturalists, including Charles Darwin, because of its vast wealth of then-unknown living species. Much was learned about how living things adapt to their environs in order to survive.

Because of its location in the heart of rain forest country, the Amazon goes through periods of heavy flooding, lapping over the banks and depositing fertile silt onto the surrounding lands. Under these conditions, agriculture and lush vegetation prosper.

A modern-day aerial shot of the Amazon.

growing trees that looked almost like palm trees, with slender silver-white trunks with enormous leaves that were covered with a down that made them gleam in the sun.

As they approached the equator, Mexia braced herself for the anticipated heat. She was pleasantly surprised by how agreeable the climate was. Cooled by the moisture from the almost-daily rain, it was nothing like the scalding dry heat she had grown up with in the southwestern United States.

"Cafe-au-lait," which means coffee with milk in French, was Mexia's description of the Amazon waters. She loved eating the fresh fish, caught in abundance each day by men in canoes. The Amazon was very low because this was the end of the dry season. The banks were often fifteen to twenty feet high. When the passengers heard a splash in the water, they would run to the side of the boat, often to see a huge slice of the tree-covered shore had fallen into the river.

At the steamer's first landing in Peru, Mexia was fascinated by the Iahuas Indians. Their dress consisted of a short skirt of split palm leaves, a cape, and armlets and anklets dyed an orange-red that shaded into their smooth brown skins: "Rather stunning they were, and quite willing to pose for their pictures in exchange for a few crackers."

On the twenty-fourth day, they arrived at Iquitos, Peru: "Iquitos is quite a lively town, sitting like a spider in the center of its web, whose silken strands are the shining rivers which come from north, west, and south,

Catching fish with bow and arrow was a common practice along the Amazon.
(Library of Congress)

traversing this wilderness. The *lanchas,* or river boats, which ascend these rivers and their affluence, carry simple necessities to exchange for skins of beast, bird and snake, for rubber and mahogany, for vegetable ivory, and for monkeys and parrots." Mexia had finally reached the end of her 2,500-mile journey up the Amazon.

Mexia stayed in Iquitos almost the entire month of October, preparing for her trip into the wilderness of the Amazon and its tributaries. She carried letters to several prominent people in the town, who were able to help her find lodging with a Peruvian family. Asking advice from several Peruvians, she learned that it was possible to continue the ascent of the Marañon River and enter the Pongo de Manseriche of the Amazon. The more she heard about the region's inaccessibility, its wildness, and its Indians, the more she wanted to go.

Mexia hired three men: Jose, who was half Peruvian and half German, as guide and hunter, and Valentino and Neptali as *cholos* (porters) and canoe men. A lancha carried them up the Marañon River. It took a week to reach Barranca, where they then transferred to a smaller craft. She and her hired men were "dumped ashore," and then the riverboat "whistled thrice, turned and slid down the river."

In Barranca, Jose tried to hire a large dugout canoe. However, while every person seemed to have his own *montaria* (small canoe), large ones were not available. Finally, he found one with four native paddlers, but it could only carry half the baggage. Mexia was tired of waiting, so she agreed to start up the river with Valentino and Neptali. Jose would follow with the rest of the baggage as soon as he could find another canoe.

Mexia relished the beauty around her: "The shining, cream-brown river, stretching from sunrise to sunset, confined by living green walls on the right and on the left, and above all the high-arched sky, delicately clouded at dawn, its intense blue relieved as the sun rose higher by fleecy white clouds, which soon piled aloft in huge cumuli, and turning black and threatening as they tore down upon us in a torrent of blinding rain, with thunder and lightning, for the afternoon storm. The deluge lessened, passed us by, traveling Andes-ward, and left us crawling in its wake refreshed and enlivened under a cloudless sky until we headed into the burning heart of a tropical sunset."

Each evening they searched out a sandy beach to

This Frederick Edwin Church painting of the Andes depicts the region's lush valleys as well as its towering, inaccessible peaks. *(Courtesy of the Granger Collection.)*

camp for the night. Valentino lit the fire and cooked. Neptali put up Mexia's cot and mosquito net, spread large Musa leaves for a rug, and then brought water for her bath. The river was too dangerous to bathe or swim in, due both to the currents and the fish and caimans— a type of crocodile six to eight feet in length. While the men worked, she roamed around the campsite, watching the birds and examining the vegetation.

They arose at dawn to "inch the canoe" upriver, battling the heavy downstream current. Huge stranded trees stuck out from the banks. The current raged past their partially submerged branches. Occasional gravel bars between islands caused shallow rapids. The men had to be careful at all times.

One of Mexia's most vivid descriptions came after seeing the Andes for the first time: "One day, as we started westward, a blue mist hung low on the horizon athwart our river highway, which, unlike other morning mists, did not dissipate with the rising sun, but took on a dim outline and a deeper blue until it dawned upon us that it was no mist, but the eastern-flung chain of the mighty Andes, the barrier that would end our journey."

One day, Mexia and her companions looked up to find the riverbank lined with Aguaruna Indians holding copper-headed spears and twelve-foot blowguns with tiny darts quite visible. Mexia and her guides were startled and frightened. These natives assumed her canoe contained Wambisas, members of a native tribe who were their blood enemies.

"When they found we were "Christianos" instead of the dreaded Wambisas, they were greatly relieved and

A group of five young Amazonian natives poses with an array of weapons in this 1923 photograph. *(Library of Congress)*

received us with rejoicing," Mexia later wrote.

In preparation for meeting the various tribes along the river, Mexia had brought presents. She presented each woman with a needle and each man with a small fishhook as goodwill gifts. Then the Indians took Mexia and her guides to the *moluca* (communal house). As in other locations, the natives were thrilled to have their pictures taken. She described them as wearing "a sort of skirt made from the wild cotton which they spin and weave, or from a fibrous bark beaten thin. The women had a kind of garment tied over one shoulder. The boys go naked."

Mexia's expedition had reached the point on the Marañon River where only canoes could go—and these slowly, either creeping from rock to rock or hauled up by ropes. When the river rose or was in flood, the rapids were immense in this narrow passage and no craft could traverse it. This was the famous Pongo de Manseriche.

They were fortunate to arrive as the river was falling, allowing them to move forward. Her paddlers were experienced river men, so they advanced easily in the dugout canoe. Mexia described the gorge as "gloomy" and dense with vegetation from top to bottom. The gorge was 330 feet deep, too deep for rapids. However, the river moved rapidly from side to side in the narrow canyon, forming ferocious whirlpools. The water welled up in standing waves and rushing crosscurrents.

Mexia established camp a few miles above the Pongo at the mouth of the Rio Santiago, whose headwaters were in the Ecuadorean Andes. The group was in the dense forest of the upper Amazon along the first and easternmost range of the Andes. She set up camp as best she could, glad when Jose and her cholos joined her a few days later. They sent the canoes and paddlers back down the river and settled in.

Soon after they encamped, the rainy season started. Mexia later wrote, "The rainy season began with unprecedented violence and the rivers rose and rose until the roar of the Pongo could be heard for miles."

She, Jose, Valentino, and Neptali camped there for three months. The heavy rains made collecting difficult. Most of it had to be done from a small canoe because of the denseness of the forest. It soon became clear that the immense rains had them trapped. Mexia realized they had to be prepared to leave.

The downpours paused in January and the floods temporarily subsided. They loaded the raft they'd made from balsa wood with Mexia's collections of plants, birds, and insects, the equipment that had survived the months of drenching, the four of them, and a tiny baby monkey Jose had acquired. Rafts were used extensively on the river system of the Upper Amazon. Because they were unwieldy, their course could only be roughly directed. A palm-leaf thatch hut was built over the platform of this raft. At the rear was a chicken coop to hold their remaining poultry. Valentino had built a fireplace, and here he prepared their meals. They loosed the vine rope holding the raft and swung out of the Santiago into the Marañon.

Valentino and Neptali handled the big oars on either side. Then they were swept into the Pongo. The raft was caught by the racing current and tossed about like a straw. A whirlpool caught them, whirled them around three times, then "spewed us out." They sped on their way safely past another great whirlpool. In twenty minutes they had raced through the most dangerous part of the river. The gorge widened. They didn't have time to think about safety. They were rapidly carried into a circling backwash that swung them around and around in spite of Valentino's and Neptali's efforts. The rocks were jagged and they had a difficult time controlling the raft. Then "a lucky thrust" pushed them out into the current once more and they floated down the river at good speed.

As dusk approached each day, the men gradually worked the raft toward the shore. Sometimes they could find places to land, other times they would be swept on down the river. A curtain and a cot would be put up for Mexia and the men would sleep on the raft's wooden floor.

As they approached Barranca, a boat came out to meet them with a huge packet of mail, some of which was nearly six months old. As Mexia read her letters and floated down the Marañon, she knew when they reached Iquitos both her raft journey and the trip up the Amazon would be finished. Her heart—despite the collection of 65,000 specimens—was heavy as she left behind a once-in-a-lifetime adventure.

EIGHT

The Tireless Adventurer

"I am not at all certain of Mrs. Mexia's next move because she isn't!"

Nina Bracelin wrote these words in a letter as Mexia was settling down in Peru, where she'd been working a few months after traveling Ecuador for over a year. The U.S. Department of Agriculture had sent her to Ecuador to find and obtain plants that control erosion, funding her entire trip. This was a welcome relief from the traditional scramble Mexia underwent securing money for each journey.

In addition to her responsibilities for the government, Mexia was determined to acquire a sample of the wax palm tree, or *palma real.* The wax palm Mexia sought grew on the Volcan de Chiles, one of the lower peaks between Ecuador and Columbia. She was interested

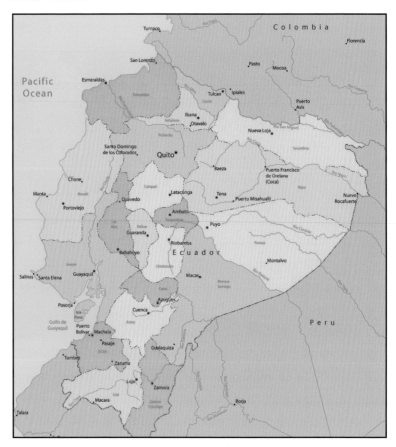

Because of the variations in elevation within Ecuador's boundaries, the climate ranges from tropical in the lowland region (La Costa) to cold and inhospitable in the highlands (La Sierra), despite being less than 150 miles apart.

because the wax palm was reported to grow at greater altitudes and to endure greater cold than any other known palm. If this were the case, it would adapt easily to California's varying locations and climates.

She called this an adventure to "Ecuador, Land of the Equator." Because her other South American equatorial trips had been in warm climates, she expected the same. Then she started up the Andes and rapidly discovered a different equatorial climate. It was cold.

Mexia found herself somewhat of a celebrity when she arrived in Ecuador. Government officials greeted her at the boat, and schools, libraries, and museums asked her to speak. She met such requests dutifully before embarking on what she truly loved: adventure.

Ecuador presented the same kinds of challenges the sixty-four-year-old Mexia had been encountering and conquering since she began seriously pursuing botany fifteen years earlier. She and her team had to navigate the Andes mountains. The weather shifted dramatically in the high altitudes, becoming quite frigid. As always, she had to adjust to a different culture, where time schedules weren't given the attention she thought they deserved, and endure the curiosities of some people who had never seen a white woman before.

Mexia got her wax palm, a major find. But the journey ended on a down note. On the return trip, she was collecting and saw some blueberries. Thinking they must be the same as in Alaska, she ate them eagerly. Immediately, she began to feel sick and dizzy. She wondered if it was the altitude. By the time her expedition reached the small-hut village of Tambo, she could barely stay astride her horse. Violent chills and pains shook her body.

The natives told her she had eaten poisonous berries. They dosed her with molasses-water and her guide, Palma, carried her to a cot. When the chills and pains increased, the natives captured a chicken and took a feather from it. Then they poked it down her throat. Soon she vomited the berries and everything else she had eaten—and the pains subsided.

Even when her experiences were dangerous or disheartening, Mexia loved being in the field. She felt fortunate to have her friend Nina Bracelin to assist in the volumes of paperwork, enabling Mexia to do more of what she loved. Bracelin, as a herbarium assistant at the University of California, worked for Mexia and for professors in the botany department. She helped one professor work up his willow collections for the revision of the genus *Salix* in the western United States. She also made a collection of exotic plants growing on an estate acquired by the university. Bracie's competent assistance meant Mexia's specimens arrived on time and in perfect condition at the herbariums, universities, and museums that ordered them.

Mexia's fame as a botanical collector had spread so that she was invited often to speak. One of her favorite topics was her trip up the Amazon. The fact that she had lived in the jungle was as fascinating to listeners as her collecting talents. They listened in awe as she described her journey across the continent of South America at its widest part. Few women had accomplished feats of this type. She was looked upon as a heroine as well as a mentor for younger women.

Both the Sierra Club and the Save-the-Redwoods League remained an important part of her life. She also tried to continue her studies at the University of California because she was, after more than a dozen years, close to a bachelor's degree.

Mexia continued to be close to the man who had helped bring her back to the world, Dr. Philip King Brown. She knew if she ever had a problem, she could call upon him. Throughout the years, Mexia wrote to him often, telling of her adventures. She also visited him and his wife each time she returned to San Francisco. When Brown died, his wife would have all of Mexia's letters retyped for posterity.

Still, speaking and even studying took second place to Mexia's first love, exploring for new specimens. In 1935, she was sixty-five years old but far more active than people twenty years younger. She still could climb steep trails, though perhaps a little more slowly and taking deeper breaths. But she was not afraid to camp with only her guides, nor to venture into regions where few women had gone. She was always eager to travel, especially in South America.

On October 1, 1935, Mexia joined Dr. Thomas H. Goodspeed and his wife in Lima, Peru, to collect in that region. He was a botanist from the University of California, Berkeley. They collected south and west of Lima. When the Goodspeeds decided to go to the southeast, Mexia left them to go north to Huanuco in the Cerro de Pasco region to collect on her own. She agreed to meet the Goodspeeds and others at Mendoza, Argentina. Her original plan had been to stay with the Goodspeeds for the duration of their trip, but collecting on her own was so important to Mexia that she had to depart.

Lake Titicaca, Bolivia, as seen from the Island of Moon in a 1915 panoramic photograph. *(Library of Congress)*

Among the specimens she searched for were the nicotianas. These tender shrubby plants are native to the Americas, with the tabacum, a type of nicotiana, as the commercial source of tobacco. The longiflora variety has white-to-purplish flowers and is found from Peru to Argentina. Her quest took her from the highlands of Peru to several destinations in southern South America.

Mexia journeyed across Lake Titicaca, the highest navigable lake in South America, by steamer and proceeded to La Paz, Bolivia, by train. The train took her to Tucuman and Mendoza in the Argentine Andes. She traveled by car via Puente de Inca, a natural bridge, to the crest of the Andes. Here she was impressed by the Christ of the Andes, a massive statue sitting atop the border between Argentina and Chile—the area known as the Uspallata Pass. The governments of both countries commissioned the statue in 1904 as a symbol of a peace treaty they had signed.

From here, Mexia knew she was close enough to fulfill another dream—traveling to the farthest point south on the continent. She took a train to Puerto Montt,

The beautiful and remote fjords of Chile remain sparsely populated to this day.
(Courtesy of Durlynn Anema.)

Chile, where she boarded the Alejandro. It was a crowded steamer going through the Chilean Fjords and the Strait of Magellan to Punta Arenas, Chile.

During the long trip, the steamer stopped only at the island of Chiloe, in southern Chile, which was a great disappointment to Mexia. She wanted to visit and explore as many places as possible and felt she had been denied this privilege. However, the fascinating scenery through the Chilean Fjords and the Strait of Magellan kept her at the ship's rail. She later wrote that this inland passage was "still more beautiful than the passage to Alaska. The innumerable islands, many of them still unexplored, are but the peaks of a submerged mountain chain and are forested to the water's edge with Nothofagus, the evergreen Southern Beech. Beneath the trees they are said to be waist-deep in spongy lichens, but I had no opportunity to land to verify this."

At one point, Alcalufes Indians paddled toward the steamer in large canoes. They wanted to barter nutria and fox skins for food, but the *Alejandro* did not stop, much to Mexia's disappointment. According to Mexia, "These were the original 'Canoe Indians', that now had dwindled to a rare few. They lived mostly in their bark canoes and carried always on a heap of sand glowing firebrands. It was due to these flickering fires seen among the countless islands and not to volcanic action that Tierra del Fuego acquired its name. They lived between the islands and along the Strait, with their diet mainly shell fish."

Letters from friends helped Mexia obtain passage to Rio Grande on the eastern coast of Tierra del Fuego. There she stayed with the manager of a big *frigorificos* (slaughterhouse). She was surprised at the many people inhabiting this place, which she thought would be an icy, uninhabited wasteland. To her eye, most inhabitants were English, Scotch, Scandinavian, or Czech. Huge *estancias* (sheep stations) dominated the region. In season, up to 5,000 or more lambs were killed each day and sent in refrigerated ships to England.

Unfortunately, the sheep had devoured almost all the vegetation. Further, Mexia was there at the end of the season and the frost had already set in, withering the flowering plants. She did enjoy the Southern Beech whose leaves had turned burnt orange, russet, and vivid crimson. She was sorry to hear the beeches were being steadily cleared off to provide more pasturage for sheep.

Because the autumn rains were about to arrive, Mexia decided to leave the mountainous area and returned to Punta Arenas, boarding the *Alejandro* for the return trip to Chile.

On June 1, 1936, she was back in Lima, Peru. She wrote, "After all Peru is perhaps the most interesting of the nations bordering the Pacific, for besides the three grand topographical regions of low, hot coast; high Sierra and Plateau; and densely forested eastern tropics, it has the remains of the vanished Indian Empires of Incas and pre-Incas."

A steamer took her to Mollendo, Peru, which she called "a forlorn little port." From there she took a train to the mountains, eagerly watching the changing scenery. "The railroad is a marvelous one. For a number of miles it runs along the beach, with the surf breaking a few feet below, then turns inland and begins to climb. As it practically never rains on this Humboldt-current-bathed coast, the hills are absolutely bare. As one rises, an occasional spindling cactus shows itself, and when the track reaches a trickle of water in a ravine, it follows this until a fair sized stream plunges down the canon along which the road winds. The mountains grow steeper and more rugged, and snow peaks peep over the shoulders of the nearer ridges, while the train thunders around countless curves," she wrote to friends.

Mexia first stopped at Cuzco, then took a train over

the pass and into the deep gorge of the Urubamba River. From there she took a bus to the town of Quillabamba. This town was several hours' ride down a narrow valley along the railroad bed. She first tried collecting near town, but cultivated fields of corn, coca, and coffee were the only vegetation. She and her guides rode horses up the river to find vegetation on the hills. She filled her press with "a beautiful rose-red bougainvillea which wreathed the streamside trees." Beside collecting, she enjoyed talking with a Dominican priest who had spent thirty years among the Machiguelo Indians and had many tales of his experiences.

When the opportunity arose to visit Machu Picchu, she went eagerly. As Mexia approached the ancient ruins, discovered in 1912, she could hardly wait for her first view. Her horse was slow, but finally she spied the buildings, "roofless but otherwise as perfect as the day when, time and reason unknown, the inhabitants last drifted away to leave their city on a hill top to the silence of the dead, to the engulfing vegetation and to the owls and snakes."

Only a day and a half was spent at this fascinating ruin. Mexia explored until dusk the first day and was up at dawn the next day. She tried to see everything and wished she could have stayed longer. But her bus back to Quillabamba was waiting.

On November 20, Mexia boarded the ship *Manezeles* for the trip to Esmeraldas, Ecuador. She was looking forward to yet another adventure. Arriving on Novem-

Machu Picchu, the fortress city of the ancient Incas, lies in a high saddle between two peaks near Cuzco, Peru. Its terraced stonework was virtually intact when rediscovered by Hiram Bingham in 1911. *(Courtesy of Art Resource.)*

ber 23, she stayed to write an article, then sent it and ninety-five Christmas cards home to San Francisco. She heard a few days would elapse before a boat could take her to Limones, Ecuador, so she unpacked cases and boxes to repack what she would need for an inland trip. She was busy sorting out her things when she was told the boat had arrived and would sail at dawn the next day.

When they reached Limones, Mexia left the boat to buy some supplies. A young boy helped carry her purchases back to the boat. As she walked back to the boat on a plank and began across the hatch, she fell through a broken board, severely injuring her leg. While the skin was not broken, her thigh took the weight of the fall and

---

MACHU PICCHU

The lost city of the Incan empire sits between two mountain peaks, 8,000 feet in the air and 2,000 feet above the Urubamba River. The site was ignored by the Spanish colonists and unknown to the larger world until American Hiram Bingham, an archaeologist, historian, and eventual U.S. Senator, rediscovered the site in 1911.

While some of the detailed features were destroyed by the Spanish, Machu Picchu remains a wonder of the world and a showcase of the advanced architectural and artistic skills of an early civilization that flourished during the fifteenth and sixteenth centuries. The Incas' skills with road building and irrigation made this isolated city a possibility. Approximately 3,000 steps link a series of terraces built over steep and rough terrain. The two hundred structures are built with blocks of granite that fit so perfectly no mortar is required.

Much of the intricate stone work, indicating that Machu Picchu was largely a spiritual compound, remains intact for travelers to visit today.

---

turned black, making walking almost impossible. As was her custom, she persevered, continuing on the boat from Limones to Concepcion. A canoe took her upriver to Playa Rica, then to her camp at El Sajedo. She stayed there from December 5 to December 28, did what collecting she could while pressing and caring for some of the thousands of plants she had collected in the preceding years, including 13,000 in Peru alone.

The reverse trip started on December 28 and culminated on January 8, 1937, when she caught a ship for the Panama Canal and San Francisco. She arrived in San

Francisco on February 5. Mexia was happy to be home—
if you could even consider her to have a home at this
point—so she could sort out her collections, give direc-
tions to Bracelin, and continue her studies.

NINE

Preserving the
Future

"I don't think there's any place in the world where a woman can't venture alone. In all my travels I've never been attacked by a wild animal, lost my way or caught a disease," Mexia told a *San Francisco News* reporter on March 6, 1937. She added, "Now that I'm back after more than two years in the wilds of South America, I find myself longing for a nice quiet jungle again."

Mexia was sixty-seven years old and still anxious to visit as many places in Mexico and South America as possible. She also wanted to finish the one course she needed for a bachelor's degree.

Bracelin had collected and saved all the letters Mexia had written that she could find. Mexia had hoped to sell an article—"Following the Sun across South America or Up the Amazon and over the Andes"—to *National Geo-*

graphic, but her dream never materialized. Parts of the article found their way into the *Sierra Club Bulletin* and *The Gull.* Mexia also published in *Bird Lore, Better Health,* and *Madrono.*

Mexia was always eager for new experiences. When she heard, in June 1937, about the biological station at the University of Michigan at Ann Arbor, she applied as a student and was quickly admitted. She spent that summer at the station in Cheboygan, Michigan. She happily presented her extensive botanical knowledge to the students, yet felt she gained even more knowledge during her stay. After her Michigan studies, she traveled to Philadelphia to visit her sister Adele, spending the end of August and part of September there.

Her sister Adele had never married and had remained in the eastern United States. Mexia hadn't seen her since May 1934, following a university lecture she had given in New York City. They maintained a correspondence throughout the years, but opportunities to see each other were rare.

The wilds still beckoned Mexia. In October, she started another trip, this time to areas around Mexico City and Oaxaca. She spent the first week traveling throughout the Mexico City area trying to collect. However, she was not feeling well and spent the next week seeing doctors and trying to recuperate. Feeling weak and tired bothered Mexia, but she was determined to overcome all signs of illness. She traveled to Toluca, Cuernavaca, Taxco, and Puebla.

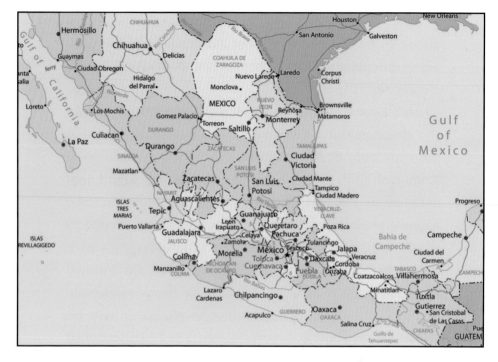

During Mexia's 1937 Mexico trip, she visited several small towns (in red) in the country's southern inland region near Mexico City before venturing once again into the Sierra Madre.

By October 26, she was feeling well enough to leave Mexico City and travel to Balsas. She traveled by canoe on the Balsas River to a mine in the state of Guerrero. The mine was quite near the coastal belt and very hot. The hills were turning brown because this was the dry season, and she found little to collect. Mexia hired a mozo, Severo, to go further into the countryside. She was pleased with her choice. He knew the country and was reliable and helpful, although slow. They collected vegetation along the streams.

In a letter to Bracelin, Mexia mentioned that it continued to be hot and dry: "I stand the heat pretty well, but it was 90 degrees in the shade this afternoon and I am much of the time in the sun and walking." The house where she stayed was at the top of a steep hill, whose climb became more difficult for her each day.

One day, as she was crossing a little river and jumping from rock to rock, her boot slipped and she went knee-deep into the water. She wrenched her right shoulder badly enough that she went to see the company doctor at the local mine. He said it was a severe sprain with no broken bones. His advice was hot applications, liniment, and taking time to rest. Each day she could raise her arm a little more, but "probably it will be complicated by rheumatism in my case," she wrote to Bracelin.

In the middle of December, Mexia arranged to go higher into the Sierra Madre. She and Severo went four days south of the mine with horses and pack mules. As they left the river basin the mountains became higher and steeper. At first, the mountains were covered with deciduous oak trees and jungle, which merged into forests of pine. At 5,400 feet, Mexia and Severo reached the last habitation. The native farmers lived in primitive conditions, yet still offered what food they had—beans and corn tortillas. Mexia wrote to Alice Eastwood, "While I lost weight I did not starve . . . the accommodations were poor [but] the country was gorgeous. There was wave after wave of the Sierra Madre range all covered with the

The maidenhair fern's genus name, *Adiantaceae,* comes from the Greek word meaning "not wetting," which refers to the fern's ability to shed water from its bright green fronds without becoming wet.

heavy, untouched pine forest and trees well up to two hundred feet high. The oaks still were present, also madronos and some other few broadleaf trees."

The collecting was scanty, but Mexia was enthralled by the adiantum, a plant commonly known as the maidenhair fern, of which she never had seen so much in her life.

Christmas was spent as any other day—collecting. Mexia wanted to go a day's journey further to Las Lumbreras, which was the site of a lost mine. However, she could find no one to take her until New Year's Day. Then a shepherd and his family, who had gone for supplies and now were returning to Las Lumbreras, agreed to guide Mexia and Severo. They packed a burro, saddled their horses, and started out.

The shepherd and his family were hospitable, sharing their food and campsite. The shepherds in that area ran mostly goats and a few sheep. They had no house and slept in the open. At night, the entire family—father, mother, and three daughters, all covered with serapes—slept right next to each other to keep warm. They invited Mexia to join them but she declined.

When she arrived at Las Lumbreras, she discovered the sheep, goats, and cattle had grazed the grass, shrubs, and low trees to the point where collecting was difficult. After a day, she and Severo decided to start back. They had been gone for five weeks, and Severo wanted to return to his family. On top of that, Mexia was beginning to feel ill again. They found mules for their packs and returned to the mine, collecting along the way. Mexia returned to Mexico City.

Although still not feeling well, she set out to collect in the Oaxaca area, south of Mexico City. She went to Mexico's Department of Forestry, Fish and Game. To her surprise, she found an old friend from childhood days— Juan Zinzer. He was thrilled to see her and took her to his superior, who gave orders she should receive all possible assistance. Then he made her an honorary member of the department.

By the end of April, Mexia's weakness had returned. She saw a doctor who said her condition was more serious than she anticipated and that she should return to California and her own physician. Before Mexia left, she took great pains to arrange all her equipment and put everything in order, expecting to return soon.

Bracelin and Dr. Brown met Mexia at the dock in San Francisco on May 29, 1938. Brown immediately put her in the hospital, where she was diagnosed with lung cancer. On July 1, Dr. Brown advised Bracelin it would be best for her to take Mexia to her home. He hoped the more pleasant atmosphere and better food would revive her. They took Mexia to Berkeley, where Bracelin lovingly cared for her. Despite all efforts, Mexia died on July 12.

A stunned Bracelin said Mexia was "like an older sister or mother to me and I shall miss her greatly."

Mexia had prepared her estate carefully, wanting her legacy to be one of environmental protection. In addition to money for her family and friends, the California Academy of Sciences was given $3,000 to pay until exhausted "the sum of one hundred dollars per month to [Nina] Bracelin so long as she shall do or perform for it botanical or other work."

Bracelin continued to work on Mexia's collections, which were incomplete at her death. Bracelin was an assistant in the botany department at the California Academy of Sciences from January 1940 to July 1943. She wrote articles about Mexia and worked closely with institutions across the world to ensure Mexia's collections were intact.

Money held in trust for her family, upon their deaths, ultimately went to the Sierra Club and the Save-the-

With the assistance of donors such as Mexia, the Save-the-Redwoods League has been able to preserve many of Northern California's majestic redwood groves. *(Library of Congress)*

Redwoods League. Her heart always remained close to these environmental organizations. The Save-the-Redwoods League received over $25,000 and used an additional $25,000 to purchase the Ynes Mexia Memorial Grove in Mendocino County, California. The Sierra Club received $20,000.

The Sierra Club passed a resolution in December 1938 saying: "Resolved that the Sierra Club, in the death of Ynes Mexia, has sustained a great loss. . . . Because of her scientific knowledge and painstaking notes, the specimens collected by her have been recognized as of exceptional value. Mrs. Mexia became a member of the Sierra Club in 1917 and went on many of its outings and, because of her cheerful disposition and extensive botanical knowledge, added materially to these expeditions."

Mexia's legacy lives on in the new genus—the *Mexianthus Mexicana*—and fifty new species named

after her, as well as the vast collections she obtained for university and museum herbariums across the world.

Ynes Mexia, the shy, lonely girl, became a worldwide name in botanical circles. Her dreams of exploration and collecting were just beginning at an age when many people retire or slow down. Age was never a factor for Mexia. She was too busy learning, leading the adventurous life few young people experience—and enjoying every minute of her time on earth.

Opposite: Ynes Mexia. *(The Bancroft Library, Berkeley)*

Timeline

1870 Born in Washington, D.C., on May 24; moves to Mexia, Texas, with parents and sister Adele.

1879 Parents separate; moves to Philadelphia, Pennsylvania, with mother and sister; attends schools in Philadelphia, Toronto, and Maryland.

1880s Moves in with father in Mexico City.

1898 Marries Herman Laue; lives with him in Tacubaya, near Mexico City.

1904 Herman Laue dies.

1908 Marries Augustin de Reygadas; lives at ranch in Tacubaya.

1909 Has mental breakdown and moves to San Francisco without de Reygadas.

1917 Joins Sierra Club and begins to go on outings.

1921 Enrolls as special student at the University of California, Berkeley.

1922 Joins a botanical expedition to Mexico from the University of California.

1924 Regains American citizenship.

1938 Returns to California on May 24 from Mexico; dies on July 12.

Mexia's expeditions

September-November 1925
Western Mexico (Sinaloa): 3,500 specimens.

August 1926-April 1927
Western Mexico (Sinaloa, Nayarit, Jalisco): at elevations up to 6,000 feet in the Sierra Madre; 33,000 specimens.

June-September 1928
Alaska (Mt. McKinley National Park—now Denali National Park and Preserve): first general collection of the park flora; 6,100 specimens.

May-July 1929
Northern and Central Mexico (Chihuahua, Mexico, Puebla, Hidalgo): 5,000 specimens.

October 1929-March 1932
South America (Brazil—Rio de Janeiro, Vicosa, Diamantina, and the state of Minas Geraes, the Amazon and other river courses in the states of Para and Amazonas; Peru—upper Amazon and Santiago river valleys.): 65,000 specimens.

September 1934-September 1935
South America (Ecuador—coastal plains and eastern Amazonian slope of Andes, northern highlands and Columbian border.): 5,000 specimens.

January 1936-January 1937
South America (Chile—southern Chile, Strait of Magellan, Tierra del Fuego; Peru—Cuzco, Machu Picchu, and Cerro del Pasco; Argentina—Tucuman and Mendoza; Ecuador—Esmeraldas.): 13,000 specimens.

October 1937-May 1938
Southwestern Mexico (Oaxaca and Guerrero): 13,000 specimens.

Glossary

angiosperms: plants with flowers; their seeds are enclosed by an ovary, a fruit.

annuals: plants that live for only one growing season.

arable land: soil fit for cultivation.

biennial: plants that live for two growing seasons.

botanist: specialist in botany or in a branch of botany.

botanical collector: a person who searches for and collects plants.

botany: a branch of biology dealing with plant life.

bulb: an underground stem modified for storage with short internodes and bearing tightly pressed, fleshy leaves.

cholos — porters

cordillera — mountain range

deciduous plants: plants that lose their leaves following the growing season each year.

division: the major taxonomic category of the plant kingdom, equivalent to the phylum of the animal kingdom.

ecology: the science of interactions among organisms and between organisms and their environment.

ecosystem: a system in which organisms and the environment interact.

epidermis: the outer cell layer of leaves and young plant organs.

escolta — military guard

estancias — sheep stations

family: a taxonomic category between order and genus.

fazenda — cattle ranch

frigorifico — slaughterhouse

fruit: a structure containing seeds — the ovary —derived at least in part from one or more flowers.

fungus: any of a major group (fungi) of saprophytic and parasitic lower plants that lack chlorophyll and include molds, rusts, mildews, smut, and mushrooms.

genus: the taxonomic category between family and species.

hacienda — ranch house

herbaceous plant: a non-woody plant.

herbarium: a collection of dried plant specimens usually mounted and systematically arranged for reference.

jacana — red-bronze bird

jacares — caimans

jepenes — biting gnats

kingdom: the most comprehensive taxonomic category.

mozo — guide

naturalist: a student of natural history, especially a field biologist.

parana — channels

parasite: an organism that lives and feeds on or in another living organism; the parasite benefits but the host is harmed.

perennials: plants that live for many growing seasons.

photosynthesis: transformation of light energy to chemical energy by green plants.

pollination: transfer of pollen from anther to stigma in angiosperms and to ovules in gymnosperms (woody plants).

population: a group of individuals of one species, capable of interbreeding.

root: any subterranean plant part.

sap: sugar-rich solution moving through phloem cells.

saprophytic: obtaining food by absorbing decayed organic material.

seed coat: the outer layer of a seed, derived from the outer layers of the ovule.

shoot: a stem and associated organs; the part of a plant above the soil.

silt: mineral particles of soil larger than clay, smaller than sand, deposited by water.

species: the taxonomic category subordinate to genus, describing populations of similar organisms.

spore: a primitive, usually unicellular, resistant or reproductive body produced by plants and capable of development into a new individual, which in some cases is unlike the parent, either directly or after fusion with another spore.

taxonomy: the science of classification.

vaqueros — cowboys

wax palm: any of several palms that yield wax; an Andean pinnate-leaved palm whose stem yields a resinous wax used in candles.

Sources

CHAPTER ONE: A Lonely Life

p. 21, "I do not think . . ." Dr. Philip King Brown to Ynes Mexia, date unknown, Ynes Mexia Collection, Bancroft Library, University of California, Berkeley.

p. 23, "To explore, enjoy . . ." Sierra Club, "Sierra Club Purposes and Goals," http://www.sierraclub.org/policy/goals.asp (accessed April 12, 2005).

CHAPTER TWO: Finding a Niche

p. 25, "I am heartily . . ." Ynes Mexia to Save-the-Redwoods League, November 3, 1919, Save-the-Redwoods League, San Francisco, CA.

p. 29, "good deal of . . ." Ynes Mexia to Alice Eastwood, July 25, 1925, Ynes Mexia Collection, California Academy of Sciences, San Francisco, CA.

CHAPTER THREE: The First Solo Expedition

p. 35, "Botany is indeed . . ." A. G. Morton, *History of Botanical Science* (London: Academic Press, 1981), vi.

p. 38, "Transporting of equipment . . ." Ynes Mexia to Dr. B. L. Robinson, July 2, 1926, Ynes Mexia Collection, Bancroft Library, University of California, Berkeley.

p. 39, "this gentleman knows . . ." Ynes Mexia, "Botanical Trails in Old Mexico—The Lure of the Unknown," *Madrono,* September 27, 1929, 227.

p. 39-40, "The streets, when . . ." Ibid.

p. 40, "it was hard . . ." Ibid.

p. 41, *"Convolvulaceae* of every . . ." Mexia, "Botanical Trails," 228.

p. 43, "Many composites were . . ." Ibid, 229.

p. 43-44, "I privately think . . ." Ynes Mexia to unknown, October 24, 1926, Ynes Mexia Collection, Bancroft Library, University of California, Berkeley.

p. 44, "keep up with . . ." Ibid.

p. 44, "Crops (and weeds) . . ." Mexia, "Botanical Trails," 230.

p. 46, "The mosquitos and . . ." Mexia, October 24, 1926.

p. 46-47, "The village was . . ." Mexia, "Botanical Trails," 230.

p. 47-48, "It was the . . ." Ynes Mexia to unknown, November 11, 1926, Ynes Mexia Collection, Bancroft Library, University of California, Berkeley.

p. 48, "The lagoons stretch . . ." Ibid.

p. 49-50, "It was eerie . . ." Ibid.

CHAPTER FOUR: Into the Sierra Madre

p. 52, "indubitable evidence . . ." Ynes Mexia to unknown, December 17, 1926, Ynes Mexia Collection, Bancroft Library, University of California, Berkeley.

p. 54, "like a silver . . ." Ibid.

p. 54, "standing on edge," Ynes Mexia, "Botanical Trails," 233.

p. 56-57, "The varieties of . . ." Ibid.

p. 57, "Talk about the primitive! . . . very welcome," Ynes Mexia to unknown, January 31, 1927, Ynes Mexia Collection, Bancroft Library, University of California, Berkeley.

p. 58, "two or three . . ." Ibid., 3.

p. 58, "Some very prickly . . ." Ibid.

p. 58, "I did not . . ." Ibid.

p. 60, "It is a great . . ." Ynes Mexia to unknown, February 28, 1927, Ynes Mexia Collection, Bancroft Library, University of California, Berkeley.

p. 61, "We did not . . ." Ibid.

p. 61, "It was a 'dip' . . ." Ibid.

p. 61, "It grew black . . ." Ibid.

p. 62-63, "just hugged the . . ." Ibid.

p. 63, "This I firmly . . ." Ibid.

p. 63, "I do not see . . ." Ibid.

p. 64, "Another like the . . . " Ynes Mexia to unknown, March 8, 1927, Ynes Mexia Collection, Bancroft Library, University of California, Berkeley.

CHAPTER FIVE: The Last American Frontier

p. 68, "most anxious to . . ." Ynes Mexia to Dr. B. L. Robinson, September 27, 1928, Ynes Mexia Collection, Bancroft Library, University of California, Berkeley.

p. 68, "I could only . . ." Ynes Mexia to Dr. Francis W. Pennell, December 10, 1928, Ynes Mexia Collection, Bancroft Library, University of California, Berkeley.

p. 69, "a novel method . . ." Ibid.

p. 70, "made no impression . . ." Ynes Mexia letter to Dr. Francis W. Pennell, September 30, 1929, Ynes Mexia Collection, Bancroft Library, University of California, Berkeley.

p. 70, "only was able . . ." Mexia to Robinson, September 27, 1928.

CHAPTER SIX: Adventure in Brazil

p. 74, "The trip down . . ." Ynes Mexia to unknown, October 15, 1929, Ynes Mexia Collection, Bancroft Library, University of California, Berkeley.

p. 75, "An imp of perversity . . . person does," Ibid.

p. 75, "as any properly . . ." Ibid.

p. 75, "I wanted to suggest . . ." Ibid.

p. 78-79, "perhaps the most . . ." Ynes Mexia to friends, November 22, 1929, Ynes Mexia Collection, Bancroft Library, University of California, Berkeley.

p. 79, "had no idea . . . scientists are," Ibid.

p. 79, "green gloom," Ibid.

p. 80, "green earth drapery," Ibid.

p. 81, "Out of the . . ." Ynes Mexia to Miss Pringle, December 16, 1929, Ynes Mexia Collection, Bancroft Library, University of California, Berkeley.

p. 83, "The village was . . ." Ynes Mexia to unknown, February 3, 1930, Ynes Mexia Collection, Bancroft Library, University of California, Berkeley.

p. 83-84, "To be in a . . ." Ibid.

p. 87, "One day I . . ." Ynes Mexia, "Glimpses of a Brazilian Cattle Ranch," (unpublished essay, April 1931, Ynes Mexia Collection, Bancroft Library, University of California, Berkeley), 4.

CHAPTER SEVEN: Up the Amazon

p. 88, "Most of us . . ." Ynes Mexia, "Three Thousand Miles up the Amazon," *Sierra Club Bulletin,* February 18, 1933, 88.

p. 90, "The river itself . . ." Ibid., 88-89.

p. 95, "Rather stunning they . . ." Ibid., 91.

p. 95-96, "Iquitos is quite . . ." Ibid., 92.

p. 97, "dumped ashore . . . the river," Ibid.

p. 97, "The shining, cream-brown . . ." Ibid.

p. 98, "inched the canoe," Ibid.

p. 98-99, "One day, as . . ." Ibid., 93.

p. 99-100, "When they found . . ." Ibid.

p. 100, "a sort of . . ." Ibid.

p. 100, "gloomy," Ynes Mexia to Dr. Bailey, April 5, 1932, Ynes Mexia Collection, Bancroft Library, University of California, Berkeley.

p. 101, "The rainy season . . ." Mexia, "Three Thousand Miles," 94.

p. 102, "spewed us out," Ibid., 95.

p. 102, "a lucky thrust," Ibid.

CHAPTER EIGHT: The Tireless Adventurer

p. 103, "I am not at all . . ." Nina Bracelin to unknown, January 8, 1936, Ynes Mexia Collection, Bancroft Library, University of California, Berkeley.

p. 104, "Ecuador, Land of . . ." Ynes Mexia, "Camping on the Equator," *Sierra Club Bulletin,* February 22, 1937, 85.

p. 109-110, "still more beautiful . . ." Ynes Mexia, "The Search for the Nicotianas," (lecture, California Academy of Sciences), 12.

p. 110, "These were the original . . ." Ibid., 13.

p. 111, "After all Peru . . ." Ynes Mexia to friends, June 1, 1936, Ynes Mexia Collection, Bancroft Library, University of California, Berkeley.

p. 111, "a forlorn little port . . ." Ibid.

p. 111, "The railroad is . . ." Ibid.

p. 112, "A beautiful rose-red . . ." Ibid.

p. 112, "roofless but otherwise . . ." Ibid., 3.

CHAPTER NINE: Preserving the Future

p. 116, "I don't think . . . jungle again," "U. C. Scientist Back from Trip Into South America for Plants," *San Francisco News*, March 6, 1937.

p. 119, "I stand the . . ." Ynes Mexia to Nina Bracelin, November 15, 1937, Ynes Mexia Collection, Bancroft Library, University of California, Berkeley.

p. 119, "probably it will . . ." Ibid.

p. 119-120, "While I lost . . ." Ynes Mexia to Alice Eastwood, February 3, 1938, Ynes Mexia Collection, Bancroft Library, University of California, Berkeley.

p. 122, "like an older . . ." Nina Bracelin to Dr. A. C. Smith, July 26, 1938, Ynes Mexia Collection, Bancroft Library, University of California, Berkeley.

p. 122, "the sum of . . ." Ynes Mexia, September 5, 1934 (last will and testament, Save-the-Redwoods League, San Francisco, CA).

p. 123, "Resolved that the . . ." "Resolution about Ynes Mexia," *Sierra Club Bulletin,* December 1938, xxix-xxx.

Bibliography

Bartram, Edwin B. "Mosses of Western Mexico Collected by Mrs. Ynes Mexia." *Journal of the Washington Academy of Science* 18 (1928): 577-82.

Bonta, Marcia Myers, ed. *American Women Afield: Writings By Pioneering Women Naturalists.* College Station: Texas A&M University Press, 1995.

Bracelin, Nina F. "Itinerary of Ynes Mexia in South America." *Madrono* 3 (1935): 174-76.

Clark, Lewis F. "Mexia Resolution." *Sierra Club Bulletin,* December 1938.

Copeland, E. B. "Brazilian Ferns Collected by Ynes Mexia." *University of California Publications in Botany 17.* Berkeley: University of California Press, 1932.

"Enricque Guillermo Antonio Mexia." The Handbook of Texas Online, University of Texas at Austin. http://www.tsha.utexas.edu/handbook/online/articles/view/MM/fme74.html.

Goerke, Heinz. *Linnaeus.* Translated by Denver Lindley. New York: Charles Scribner's Sons, 1973.

Goodspeed, Thomas H. *Plant Hunters in the Andes.* Berkeley: University of California Press, 1961.

Goodspeed, Thomas H. and H. E. Stark. *University of California Publications in Botany 28l.* Berkeley: University of California Press, 1955.

James, Edward T., ed. *Notable American Women, 1607-1950.* Cambridge, MA: Harvard University Press, 1971.

McLoone, Margo. *Women Explorers in North and South America.* Mankato, MN: Capstone Press, 1997.

Mexia, Ynes. "Bird Study for Beginners." *Bird Lore* 27 (1925): 68-72, 137-141.

———. "Birds of Brazil." *The Gull,* July/August 1930.

———. "Botanical Trails in Old Mexico—The Lure of the Unknown." *Madrono* 1 (September 27, 1929): 227-38.

———. "Camping on the Equator." *Sierra Club Bulletin* 22 (February 1937): 85-91.

———. Collected Letters. Ynes Mexia Collection, Bancroft Library, University of California, Berkeley.

———. "Down the San Pedro River." *The Gull*, December 1926.

———."Experiences in Hospitable Mexico." *Better Health,* October 1927, 432-58.

———. "Glimpses of a Brazilian Cattle Ranch." (unpublished, Ynes Mexia Collection, Bancroft Library, University of California, Berkeley, April 1931).

———. "Ramphastidae." *The Gull,* July 1933.

———. "Three Thousand Miles up the Amazon." *Sierra Club Bulletin* 18 (February 1933): 88-96.

———. "Vignettes of Birds Long Since Flown." *The Gull,* June 1935.

Minnesota State University at Mankato. "Machu Picchu." http://www.mnsu.edu/emuseum/prehistory/latinamerica/south/sites/machu_picchu.html.

Morton, A. G. *History of Botanical Science.* London: Academic Press, 1981.

National Park Service. "Denali." U.S. Department of the Interior. http://www.nps.gov/dena/.

Shearer, Benjamin F. and Barbara S. Shearer, eds. *Notable Women in the Life Sciences: A Biographical Dictionary.*

Westport, CT: Greenwood Press, 1996.

Tyler-Whittle, Michael. *The Plant Hunters.* Philadelphia: Chilton Book Company, 1970.

"U. C. Scientist Back from Trip into South America for Plants." *San Francisco News*, March 6, 1937.

"Woman Braves Amazon Wilds for Specimens." *San Francisco Chronicle*, March 22, 1932.

Yount, Lisa. *A to Z of Women in Science and Math.* New York: Facts on File, Inc., 1999.

Web sites

http://www.botany.org/
The official Web site of the Botanical Society of America.

http://www.savetheredwoods.org/
The official Web site of the Save-the-Redwoods League.

http://www.sierraclub.org/
The official Web site of the Sierra Club.

Index